Irish Family History on t

A Directory

Stuart A. Raymond

Published by:
Federation of Family History Societies (Publications) Ltd.,
Units 15-16, Chesham Industrial Centre,
Oram Street, Bury,
Lancashire, BL9 6EN, U.K.

in association with
S.A. & M.J.Raymond,
P.O.Box 35,
Exeter,
EX1 3YZ
Phone (01392) 252193
Email: stuart@samjraymond.softnet.co.uk
Webpage: www.soft.net.uk/samjraymond.igb.htm

Copyright © Stuart A. Raymond

ISBNs:
Federation of Family History Society: 1-86006-147-8
S.A. & M.J.Raymond: 1-899668-20-9

First published 2001

Printed and bound by Oxuniprint, Great Clarendon Street, Oxford OX2 6DP

Contents

	Introduction	4
1.	Gateways, Search Engines, *etc.*	5
2.	General Introductions to Irish Genealogy	6
3.	Libraries, Record Offices, and Books	8
4.	Family History Societies	14
5.	Discussion Groups: Mailing Lists and Newsgroups	16
6.	Message / Query Boards	21
7.	County Pages	26
8.	Surnames	34
9.	Sources	37
10.	Occupational Records	58
11.	Miscellaneous Sites	59
12.	Professional Services, Booksellers, *etc.*	63
	Subject Index	65
	Institution Index	67
	Place Index	69

Introduction

A vast amount of information concerning genealogy and family history is now available on the internet. Surfing the net can be a very productive process for the researcher; it can, however, also be very frustrating. There are thousands of genealogical web sites worth visiting, but the means for finding particular relevant sites are very poor. Search engines frequently list dozens of relevant sites, but not the ones required. 'Gateway' sites are not always easy to use. Links are not always kept up to date. It is easy for relevant sites to escape attention.

I hope that this directory will provide at least a partial means for overcoming these problems. It is intended to help you identify those sites most relevant to your research. The listing is, inevitably, selective. I have only included those sites likely to provide you with useful information. Sites devoted to particular families are excluded: a listing would occupy at least a whole volume. I have also excluded passenger list sites dealing with single voyages: again, a full listing would be extensive. Sites of general interest, e.g. search engines, maps, *etc.*, are also excluded. Many of the sites I have listed, and especially those in chapters 1, 7 and 8, can be used to find sites excluded from this directory.

Beginners should also consult:
CHRISTIAN, PETER. *Finding genealogy on the internet.* David Hawgood, 1999. This book offers many suggestions to help you improve your surfing techniques.

It should be noted that **http:** should be prefixed to all URLs in this directory.

This listing is as up-to-date as I have been able to make it. However, new web pages are being mounted every day, and URLs change frequently. Consequently, it is anticipated that this directory will need frequent updating. If you are unable to find a site listed here, then you should check Cyndis List or one of the other gateways listed in chapter 1; the probability is that the site has moved to another address. Alternatively, search words from the title - or the URL - on a search engine such as www.google.com. It is frequently the case that sites which have not been found directly can be found in this way.

If you know of sites which have not been listed here, or which are new, please let me know so that they may be included in the next edition of this directory.

My thanks go to Cynthia Hanson, who has typed most of this book, to Bob Boyd, who has seen it through the press, and to the officers of the Federation of Family History Societies, who accepted it for publication.

1. Gateways, Search Engines etc.

There are a variety of gateways and search engines for Irish genealogists. One of the most useful is Genuki, which itself provides a great deal of general information. Cyndis list is the major international gateway; it has an American bias, but nevertheless provides numerous links to Irish sites. Quite a number of sites offer similar help, although the 'international' ones tend to be biased towards U.S. genealogy. General search engines are not listed here; they may be found on Cyndis List, or by accessing some of the other sites listed below.

- Genuki Ireland
  www.genuki.org.uk/big.irl
- Genuki Book by David Hawgood
  www.hawgood.co.uk/genuki/index.htm

A useful description of Genuki contents, also published in book format as AWGOOD, DAVID. *Genuki: UK and Ireland Genealogy on the Internet*. David Hawgood / Federation of Family History Societies, 2000.

- Cyndis List of Genealogy Sites on the Internet: Ireland & Northern Ireland
  www.cyndislist.com/ireland.htm

The most extensive listing of genealogical websites on the internet, which has also been published in book format: HOWELLS, CYNDI. *Cyndis's list: a comprehensive list of 40,000 genealogy sites on the Internet*. Baltimore: Genealogical Publishing, 1999.

- Roots Web Genealogical Data Cooperative
  www.rootsweb.com

Home to thousands of genealogical mailing lists, the Genweb project, web sites, *etc., etc*. American bias, but also of Irish interest.

- Ireland Genealogical Projects: The Original Ireland Gen Web Project
  www.rootsweb.com/~irlwgw/

Lists county pages, query pages, *etc*.

See also:
- Ireland Gen Web
  www.irelandgenweb.com/

There are a variety of other gateway sites:

- The Celtic Connection
  www.geocities.com/Heartland/Prairie/8088/ire.html

Gateway mainly to county websites

- Genealogy Ireland-Eire-History
  www.members.tripod.com/~Caryl-Williams/Eire-7.html

- Genealogy Northern Ireland
  www.aboutye.com/local/genealogy.html

- Helm's Genealogy Toolbox: Ireland
  www.genealogytoolbox.com/ireland.html

Gateway

- Ireland: Irish Genealogy Pages
  www.scotlandsclans.com/ireland.htm

- Irish Ancestral Pages
  www.geocities.com/irishancestralpages

Includes various databases

- Irish Genealogy: Andrew J. Morris
  www.genealogy.org/~ajmorris/ireland/ireland.htm

- Irish Genealogy Links
  www.geocities.com/SiliconValley/Haven/1538/irish.html

- Ireland Genealogy Links & Chat
  www.100megsfree.@com/gen/ire.html
Gateway to County links

- Irish Genealogy on the Net
  irishgenealogy.net/
New gateway.

- Irish Genealogy on the Web
  www.io.com/~abrieal/irishgen/

- Irish Insight: The A to Z of Irish Genealogy
  www.irish-insight.com/a2z-genealogy

- Irish Resources on the Internet
  www.genealogy.com/30__links.html
Brief introduction

- My Irish Ancestry.com
  www.myirishancestry.com/

- UK Genealogy.Ireland Research
  www.ukgenealogy.co.uk/ireland.htm
Covers Eire and Northern Ireland

Many Irish genealogical sites may be found by commencing at one of:

- Discover Ireland Genealogy Web Ring
  www.accessgenealogy.com/rings/ire

- Discover Northern Ireland Genealogy Webring
  www.accessgenealogy.com/rings/nire/index.htm

For a gateway to Irish genealogy in Canada, visit:

- Irish Genealogy in Canada
  layden-zella.tripod.com/IrishGen.index.html

If you want to place your research in the wider context of Irish history, see:

- Irish History on the Web
  www.vms.utexas.edu/~jdana/irehist.html

2. General Introduction to Genealogy

Numerous general guides to Irish genealogy are available on the internet; most provide similar basic guidance. Many family history society sites (chapter 4 below) have beginners' guides; so do many of the county pages listed in chapter 7. Some of the pages listed below are extensive - especially those from major institutions.

- Centre for Irish Genealogical and Historical Studies
  homepage.tinet.ie/~seanjmurphy
Includes 'Directory of Irish genealogy', *etc.*

- Family Search Ireland Research Guidance
  www.familysearch.org/Eng/Search/RG/frameset__rg.asp.
Guide from the Latter-Day Saints - select 'Ireland'

- Fianna Guide to Irish Genealogy
  www.rootsweb.com/~fianna
Extensive, including county pages

- Finding your Ancestors in Ireland
  www.genealogy.com/4__pocket.html?Welcome=991304731
Includes notes on how to do it from overseas

- From Ireland
  www.from-ireland.net
Extensive new site

- Genealogy of the Isles: Ireland
  www.io.com/~crberry/isles/index__ireland.html

- Irish
  www.genealogy.com/00000374.html
Brief introduction

- Irish Abroad
  www.irishabroad.com/YourRoots/

- Irish Ancestors
  scripts.ireland.com/ancestor/

- Irish Ancestors: Irish Times
  www.ireland.com/ancestor/

One of the best sites; hundred of pages

- Irish Ancestors.net
  freepages.genealogy.rootsweb.com/~irishancestors/

- Irish Genealogy: search for your roots
  www.goireland.com/Genealogy/

- Irish Research
  www.genalogy.com/4__irsrcs.html

Brief introduction

- Local Ireland
  www.local.ie/genealogy

Numerous pages; includes messageboard, surname origins, Irish family register, email newsletter etc.

- Shamrock Genealogy
  community-2.webtv.net/shamrockroots

- Tracing your roots in Ireland
  www.shopshamrock.com/genealogy/

Brief introductory notes with link to bookshop etc.

- Seventeenth Century Sources
  freepages.genealogy.rootsweb.com/~irishancestors/Add17.html

Introduction to *Inquisitions Post Mortem,* Patent Rolls, various muster rolls, tax lists, *etc. etc.*

- Eighteenth Century Sources
  freepages.genealogy.rootsweb.com/~irishancestors/Add18.html

Covers a wide range of sources

- Nineteenth Century Sources
  freepages.genealogy.rootsweb.com/~irishancestors/Add19.html

Covers a wide range of sources, including estate records, wills, poor law records, *etc. etc.*

- A little bit of Ireland
  home.att.net/~labaths

Mainly transcriptions of original sources

- Irish Records Extractions Database
  www.ancestry.com/search/rectype/inddbs/3876.htm

Index of numerous diverse sources; 100,000+ records

- Irish Records Index, 1500-1920
  www.ancestry.com/search/rectype/inddbs/4077.htm

Index to a collection held by the Mormon's Family History Library

3. Libraries, Record Offices and Books

Most of the information sought by genealogists is likely to be found in books and archival sources. The libraries and record offices which hold these resources provide an essential genealogical service, which is unlikely to be replaced by the internet. The value of the latter is in pointing you in the right direction, and helping you to identify the books and records you need to check. Many libraries and record offices now have webpages, listed here. Those which provide internet access to their catalogues are providing a particularly valuable service.

It is impossible here to provide a complete list of library and record office websites likely to be of use to genealogists. Such a list would have to include most public and university libraries, and is outside the scope of this book. However, a number of sites provide extensive listings. Three sites are specifically intended for genealogists:

- Familia: the UK and Ireland's guide to genealogical resources in public libraries
  www.earl.org.uk/familia/
- Local Library (Republic of Ireland)
  scripts.ireland.com/ancestor/browse/addresses/librarya__l.htm

Continued at /librarym-z.htm
List of addresses

- Local Library (Northern Ireland
  scripts.ireland.com/ancestor/browse/addresses/libraryn.htm

There are also a number of general gateways to library sites:
- Consortium of University Research Libraries
  www.curl.ac.uk

Resources of libraries throughout the British Isles

- Libdex: the Library Index. Ireland
  www.libdex.com/country/Ireland.html
- Libdex: the Library Index. Northern Ireland
  www.libdex.com/country/Northern__Ireland.html

For university library catalogues, consult:
- Irish Academic Library Catalogues
  www.may.ie/library/file__03.htm

List

- Hytelnet: 1st Directory of Internet Resources. Library Catalogs: Ireland
  www.lights.com/hytelnet/ie0/ie000.html

University Libraries

For a union catalogue of 20 UK and Irish university libraries, consult:
- Copac
  www.copac.ac.uk

For record offices, consult:
- Major Repositories
  scripts.ireland.com/ancestor/browse/addresses/major.htm

List

- Archon: Historical Manuscripts Commission
  www.hmc.gov.uk/archon/archon.htm

Includes lists of repositories in Northern Ireland and the Republic of Ireland

See also:
- Historical Manuscripts Commission: Sources for Genealogy
  www.hmc.gov.uk/nra/browser/browserhome.htm

Major Institutions

British Library

- The British Library
  www.bl.uk

General Information

- The British Library Public Catalogue
  blpc.bl.uk

Book catalogue

- British Library Manuscripts Catalogue
  molcat.bl.uk/

Extensive Irish collection

Family History Library

- Family History Library
  www.familysearch.org

Library of the Latter Day Saints

- Family History Centres
  www.familysearch.org/eng/Library/FHC/frameset_fhc.asp

- LDS films of interest to those studying Co. Longford families
  personal.nbnet.nb.ca/tmoffatt/ldsfilms.html

- FHC Film and Microfilm
  www.exis.net/ahd/monaghan/fhc-records.htm

For Co. Monaghan

Linen Hall Library

- Linen Hall Library, Belfast
  www.linenhall.com

The leading centre for Irish and local studies in the north of Ireland. Includes catalogue

National Archives of Ireland

- A Guide to the National Archives of Ireland
  homepages.circom.net/~seanjmurphy/nai/

- National Archives of Ireland
  www.nationalarchives.ie

- National Archives of Ireland: Genealogy
  www.nationalarchives.ie.genealogy.html

National Library of Ireland

- National Library of Ireland
  www.nli.ie

Includes catalogue, pages on 'family history research' in the National Library, details of collections, *etc.*

Public Record Office

- Irish Genealogy
  www.pro.gov.uk/leaflets/ri2063.htm

Resources in the UK Public Record Office

- Public Record Office
  www.pro.gov.uk

Public Record Office of Northern Ireland

- The Public Record Office of Northern Ireland
  proni.nics.gov.uk/

Includes page on 'How to trace your family tree', 'understanding the stones' (i.e. monumental inscriptions), and details of the extensive records held

Representative Church Body Library

- Representative Church Body Library
  www.ireland.anglican.org/library/library.html

Repository of the archives of the Church of Ireland

Overseas Institutions

Balch Institute

- The Balch Institute for Ethnic Studies
  www.balchinstitute.org

The Institute (in Philadelphia) holds various collections relating to Irish and Scotch Irish in America

- The Ulster American Folk Park
  www.folkpark.com
Includes 'The Centre for Migration Studies', with its library and 'emigration database'

University Libraries

- Boole Library, University College Cork, Ireland: Special Collections
  booleweb.ucc.ie/search/subject/speccol/speccol.htm

- University of Dublin. Trinity College
  www.tcd.ie/library

- National University of Ireland, Maynooth
  www.may.ie/library

- University of Ulster Library Services
  www.ulst.ac.uk/library/

Public Libraries

Clare

- Clare Library
Local Studies Centre
  www.clarelibrary.ie/eolas/library/local-studies/locstudi1.htm

- Clare County Library
  www.clarelibrary.ie
Many pages, some listed elsewhere in this directory

Cork

- Cork Archives Institute
  www.corkcorp.ie/facilities/facilities__archive.html

Donegal

- Donegal County Library
  www.donegal.ie/library/default.htm
Includes page on 'Donegal Studies'

Dublin

- Dublin City Public Libraries
  www.ie/resource/dublincity/library/
Click the 'Cultural Heritage' icon for 'Genealogy' and 'Dublin City Archives'. It is also planned to mount the library's catalogue on the web

- Sources for Family History
  www.iol.ie/dublincitylibrary/gafamily.htm
In Dublin City Library

- Sources for the History of Dublin and Ireland
  www.iol.ie/dublincitylibrary/gasources.htm
In Dublin City Library

- Dun Laoghaire-Rathdown County Council Public Library Service: Local History Department
  www.dircoco.ie/library/lhistory.htm
Includes page on genealogical resources

- Fingal County Libraries
  www.iol.ie/~fincolib
Includes pages on 'Local Studies' and 'County Archives'

Galway

- Galway Public Library
  www.galwaylibrary.ie
Includes page on 'archives' in the local studies dept.

Kildare

- Kildare Heritage & Genealogy Co.
  Kildare.ie/library/KildareHeritage/page2.html

- Genealogical Sources
  Kildare.ie/library/KildareHeritage/page3.html
At Kildare Heritage and Genealogy Co.

- Kildare Library & Art Services: Kildare Local Studies Department
  kildare.ie/library/localstudies.htm

Kilkenny
- Kilkenny County Library
  www.earl.org.uk/familia/services/eire/kilkenny.html

Limerick
- Limerick City Public Libraries
  www.limerickcorp.ie/librarymain.htm
Includes brief bibliography of Limerick history - click on 'local studies'

Longford
- Longford County Library
  longford.local.ie/content/9837.shtml

Mayo
- Library Service for County Mayo
  www.mayo-ireland.ie/Mayo/CoDev/MayoLibs.htm
Includes pages on 'genealogy' and 'history'

Meath
- Archives and Libraries for Genealogical and Local Historical Research concerning County Meath
  www.angelfire.com/ak2/ashbourne/archives.html

Monaghan
- Public Libraries in County Monaghan
  homepages.tinet.ie/~monaghan/libbra.htm
Includes pages on 'Genealogy in County Monaghan' and 'History of local towns'

Roscommon
- Roscommon County Library
  www.iol.ie/~roslib/
Includes page on 'local history'

Tipperary
- Tipperary Heritage Unit
  www.iol.ie/~thu

- Tipperary Libraries: Local Studies Department
  ireland.iol.ie/%7Etipplibs/Local.htm

Wexford
- Wexford Public Libraries Local Studies Service
  www.wexford.ie/local.htm

Irish Family History Foundation
This Foundation coordinates a network of government sponsored genealogical research centres which have computerised millions of records. These centres are listed here. The coordinating body is:

- Irish Family History Foundation
  www.irishroots.net

- Report on the Irish Heritage Centres Customer Satisfaction Survey
  tiara.ie/results.htm

For listings of the centres, see:
- County Based Genealogical Centres
  www.nationalarchives.ie/genealogy__countycentres.html

- Local Heritage Centres
  scripts.ireland.com/ancestor/browse/addresses/heritagea-h.htm
  Continued at /heritagel-z.htm

Antrim
- Ulster Historical Foundation
  www.irishroots.net/AntmDown
Covers Co. Antrim and Co. Down

Armagh
- County Armagh Genealogy: Armagh Ancestry
  www.irishroots.net/Armagh.htm

Carlow
- Carlow Research Centre
  www.irishroots.net/Carlow.htm

Clare
- Clare Heritage and Genealogical Centre
  clare.irish-roots.net/

Cork
- Mallow Heritage Centre
  www.irishroots.net/Cork.htm
Covers Co. Cork

Donegal
- Donegal Ancestry
  www.irishroots.net/Donegal.htm

Down
See Antrim

Dublin
- Genealogy in Dublin, Ireland
  www.irishroots.net/Dublin.htm

Fermanagh
- Heritage World
  www.irishroots.net/FnghTym.htm
Covers Co. Fermanagh and Co. Tyrone

Galway
- Genealogy in Galway in the West of Ireland
  www.irishroots.net/Galway.htm

Kerry
- Killarney Genealogical Centre
  www.irishroots.net/Kerry.htm
Covers Co. Kerry

Kildare
Kildare Heritage and Genealogy Company
  www.irishroots.net/Kildare.htm

Kilkenny
- Kilkenny Ancestry
  www.irishroots.net/Kilkenny.htm

Laois
- Laois & Offaly Family History Research Centre
  www.irishroots.com/LaoisOff.htm

- Irish Midlands Ancestry
  www.irishmidlandsancestry.com
Covers Laois and Offaly

Leitrim
- Leitrim Genealogy Centre
  www.irishroots.net/Leitrim.htm

Limerick
- Limerick Ancestry
  www.irishroots.net/Limerick.htm

Londonderry
- County Derry or Londonderry Genealogy Centre
  www.irishroots.net/Derry.htm

Longford
- Longford Research Centre
  www.irishroots.net/Longford.htm

Louth
See Meath

Mayo
- Mayo Family History Research Centres
  mayo.irishroots.net/mayo.htm

Meath
- Meath Heritage Centre
  www.irishroots.net/Meath.htm

- Meath-Louth Family Research Centre
  www.irishroots.net/Louth.htm

Monaghan

- Monaghan Research Centre
  www.irishroots.net/Monaghan.htm

Offaly

See Laois

Roscommon

- County Roscommon Heritage and Genalogy Society
  www.irishroots.net/Roscmmn.htm

Sligo

- County Sligo Heritage and Genealogy Centre
  www.irishroots.net/Sligo.htm

Tipperary

- Genealogy in Tipperary
  www.irishroots.net/Tipp.htm
- Bru Boru Heritage Centre
  www.irishroots.net/STipp.htm

Covers South Tipperary

- The Tipperary North Family Research Centre
  www.irishroots.net/NTipp.htm

Tyrone

See Tipperary

Waterford

- Waterford Research Centre
  www.irishroots.net/Waterford.htm

Westmeath

- Dun na Si Heritage Centre
  www.irishroots.net/Westmeath.htm

Covers Co. Westmeath

Wexford

- Wexford Genealogy Centre
  www.irishroots.net/Wexford.htm

Wicklow

- Wicklow Research Centre
  www.irishroots.net/Wicklow.htm

No information on this site at the time of writing

Books

It is vital that the genealogist should be aware of the thousands of published books that may be of assistance in research. They contain far more information than is available on the web. The Northern Irish genealogist is fortunate that a number of useful web-based bibliographies are available; these are listed here. Once you have identified the particular books you need, you can find them by checking the library catalogues listed earlier in this chapter.

- Guide to Further Reading
  www.nationalarchives.ie/genealogy4.html
- Sources of Research in Irish Genealogy
  lcweb.loc.gov/rr/genealogy/bib__guid/ireland.html

Library of Congress bibliography compiled in 1998

- The Irish Ancestral Research Associaton: Books, Publications and Libraries
  tiara.ie/books.html

Details of books for sale, libraries, publishers, periodicals, etc.

- Northern Irish References: Ulster Province Family History
  members.aol.com/Manus/ulsterref.html

Bibliographic guide

Antrim

- Antrim
  members.aol.com/Manus/nirantrim.html

Bibliography

Armagh
- Armagh
   members.aol.com/Manus/nirarmagh.html

   Bibliography

Donegal
- Donegal
   members.aol.com/Manus/nirdonegal.html

   Bibliography

Down
- Down
   members.aol.com/Manus/nirdown.html

   Bibliography

Fermanagh
- Fermanagh
   members.aol.com/Manus/nirfermanagh.html

   Bibliography

Londonderry
- Derry
   members.aol.com/Manus/nirderry.html

   Bibliography

Monaghan
- Monaghan
   members.aol.com/Manus/nirmonaghan.html

   Bibliography

Sligo
- County Sligo, Ireland: Books
   www.rootsweb.com/%7Eirlsli/books.html

   Lists books with purchasing details

Tyrone
- Tyrone
   members.aol.com/Manus/nirtyrone.html

   Bibliography

4. Family History Societies

Many Irish family history societies have websites. These generally provide information on the society — names of officers, meetings, membership information, publications, services offered, lists of members' interests, links to other web pages, *etc.* A number of listings of societies are available:

- Family History and Genealogy Societies: Ireland
   www.genuki.org.uk/Societies/Ireland

- Family History Societies
   scripts.ireland.com/ancestor/browse/addresses/family.htm
   Brief list

- Federation of Family History Societies: Irish Societies
   www.ffhs.org.uk/General/Members/Ireland.htm
   Lists addresses

- Local Family History Societies in Ireland
   www.iol.ie/~inshrts/Societies.html

Brief notes on various societies

For local history societies, see:
- Local History Societies
   scripts.ireland.com/ancestor/browse/addresses/history.htm
   List

National & Regional Organisations

- Council of Irish Genealogical Organisations
   indigo.ie/~gorry/CIGO.html

- Genealogical Society of Ireland
   www.dun-laoghaire.com/genealogy

- Irish Family History Society
  homepage.eircom.net/~ifhs/
- North of Ireland Family History Society
  www.nifhs.org
- Ulster Historical Foundation
  www.ancestryireland.com

Overseas Societies

- Irish Genealogical Society Int'l
  www.rootsweb.com/~Irish

Based in Minneapolis area, Minnesota

- American Irish Historical Society
  www.aihs.org
- Irish American Archives Society
  ohioaoh.freeyellow.com/iaas.htm

Irish emigrants to Cleveland, Ohio

- The Irish Ancestral Heritage Centre
  tiara.ie

Based in Massachusetts

- Irish Family History Forum
  www.ifhf.org

Based in New York

- Irish Genealogical Society of Michigan
  www.rootsweb.com/~miigsm/
- Irish Genealogical Society of Wisconsin
  www.execpc.com/~igsw/
- Buffalo Irish Genealogical Society
  www.buffalonet.org/army/bigs.htm
- Irish Palatine Association
  www.local.ie/content/28303.shtml

For German migrants to Ireland

Local Organisations

Cork

- Cork Genealogical Society
  homepage.tinet.ie/%7Eaocoleman
- Mallow Archaeological & Historical Society
  www.rootsweb.com/~irlmahs/

For northern Co. Cork

Galway

- East Galway Family History Society
  www.mayo-ireland.ie/Geneal/EtGalway.htm
- West Galway Family History Society
  www.mayo.ireland.ie/Geneal/WtGalway.htm
- Western Family History Association
  www.galwayadvertiser.ie/IFHS/index.html

Based in Galway

Offaly

- Offaly Historical & Archaeological Society
  www.offalyhistory.com/index.html

Roscommon

- County Roscommon Family History Society
  www.geocities.com/Heartland/Pines/7030

Tipperary

- Cumann Staire Chontae Thiobraid Arann / County Tipperary Historical Society
  www.iol.ie/~tipplibs/Welcome.htm

5. Discussion Groups: Mailing Lists and Newsgroups

Want to ask someone who knows? Then join one of the groups listed here. For general information on mailing lists, visit:

- FAQ: Mailing Lists: What are they for?
  helpdesk.rootsweb.com/help/mail1.html

When you join a mailing list, you can send and receive messages from every other member of the group. By way of contrast, you do not have to join the Usenet newsgroups in order to use them; all you need is newsreading software. The two major Irish newsgroups are 'gatewayed' to, and can also be used as, mailing lists. They are:

- soc.genealogy.ireland
  Gatewayed to Genire (see below)

- soc.genealogy.surnames.ireland
  www.rootsweb.com/~surnames/ireland-intro
  Gatewayed to IRL-SURNAMES (see below)

An index to the contents of newsgroups is available at:
- Deja's Usenet Archive
  groups.google.com/googlegroups/deja_announcement.html

The most comprehensive listing of mailing lists is:
- Genealogy Resources on the Internet: Ireland mailing lists
  www.rootsweb.com/~jfuller/gen_mail_country-ire.html

See also
- Genealogy Mailing Lists
  www.genuki.org.uk/indexes/MailingLists.html

- Mailing Lists
  lists.rootsweb.com

General Irish Mailing Lists

- All-things-Irish Mailing List
  lists.rootsweb.com/index/other/Ethnic_Irish/ALL-THINGS-IRISH.html

- Fianna Mailing List
  lists5.rootsweb.com/index/intl/IRL/FIANNA.html

- Genire Mailing List
  lists5.rootsweb.com/index/intl/IRL/GENIRE.html

- Gen-Trivia Ireland
  lists5.rootsweb.com/index/intl/IRL/GEN-TRIVIA-IRELAND.html

- Ireland GenWeb Mailing List
  lists5.rootsweb.com/index/intl/IRL/IrelandGenWeb.html

- Ireland Mailing List
  lists5.rootsweb.com/index/intl/IRL/IRELAND.html

- Ireland-Roots Mailing List
  lists5.rootsweb.com/index/intl/IRL/IRELAND-ROOTS.html

- irishancestry
  groups.yahoo.com/irishancestry

- IrishGenes Mailing List
  lists5.rootsweb.com/index/intl/IRL/IrishGenes.html

- Shamrock Mailing List
  lists5.rootsweb.com/index/intl/IRL/SHAMROCK.html

Irish Overseas Mailing Lists

- Aus-Irish Mailing List
  lists.rootsweb.com/index/other/Ethnic-Irish/AUS-IRISH.html

- Irish Australian
  groups.yahoo.com/group/irishaustralian

- Can-Montreal Mailing List
  lists.rootsweb.com/index/other/Ethnic-Irish/CAN-MONTREAL-IRISH.html

- Irish American Obituaries
  lists.rootsweb.com/index/other/Ethnic-Irish/IRISH-AMERICAN-OBITUARIES.html

- OH-Cleveland-Irish Mailing List
  lists.rootsweb.com/index/other/Ethnic-Irish/OH-CLEVELAND-IRISH.html

- IA-Irish Mailing List
  lists.rootsweb.com/index/other/Ethnic-Irish/IA-IRISH.html
  For Irish in Iowa

Specialist Mailing Lists

- Anglo-Irish
  groups.yahoo.com/group/AngloIrish

- Ireland Book-Discussion Mailing List
  lists5.rootsweb.com/index/intl/IRL/IRELAND-BOOKS-DISCUSSION.html

- Ireland Cemeteries Mailing List
  lists5.rootsweb.com/index/intl/IRL/IRELAND-CEMETERIES.html

- IRL-CLANS Mailing List
  lists5.rootsweb.com/index/intl/IRL/IRL-CLANS.html

- IRL-PALATINE Mailing List
  lists5.rootsweb.com/index/intl/IRL/IRL-PALATINE.html

- Irish-Famine Mailing List
  lists5.rootsweb.com/index/intl/IRL/IRISH-FAMINE.html

- FENIANS Mailing List
  lists5.rootsweb.com/index/intl/IRL/FENIANS.html

- Ireland Obits Mailing List
  lists5.rootsweb.com/index/intl/IRL/IRELAND-OBITS.html

- Irish-Adoptees-Search Mailing List
  lists5.rootsweb.com/index/intl/IRL/IRISH-ADOPTEES-SEARCH.html

- Irishgenealogicalproject
  groups.yahoo.com/group/irishgenealogicalproject

- IRL-SURNAMES Mailing List
  lists5.rootsweb.com/index/intl/IRL/IRL-SURNAMES.html
  Gatewayed to soc.genealogy.surnames.ireland (see above)

- Scotch-Irish Mailing List
  lists5.rootsweb.com/index/intl/NIR/Scotch-Irish.html

- Transcriptions Eire Mailing List
  lists5.rootsweb.com/index/intl/IRL/TRANSCRIPTIONS-EIRE.html

Provincial Mailing Lists

Connaught

- IRL-CONNAUGHT Mailing List
  lists5.rootsweb.com/index/intl/IRL/IRL-CONNAUGHT.html

Leinster

- IRL-LEINSTER Mailing List
  lists5.rootsweb.com/index/intl/IRL/IRL-LEINSTER.html

Ulster/Northern Ireland

- IRL-Ulster Mailing List
  lists.rootsweb.com/index/intl/NIR/IRL-ULSTER.html

- Northern Ireland Mailing List
  lists.rootsweb.com/index/intl/NIR/NORTHERN-IRELAND.html

- Northern Ireland Gen Web Mailing List
  lists.rootsweb.com/index/intl/NIR/NorthernIrelandGenWeb.html
- Unionist-Culture Mailing List
  lists.rootsweb.com/index.intl/NIR/Unionist-Culture.html
  Covers Northern Ireland
- N-Ireland Mailing List
  lists.rootsweb.com/index/intl/NIR/N-IRELAND.html

County & Local Mailing Lists

Antrim
- Co. Antrim Mailing List
  mcfaul.jumpbusiness.com
- IRL-Antrim Mailing List
  lists5.rootsweb.com/index/intl/NIR/IRL-ANTRIM.html
- NIR-Antrim Mailing List
  lists5.rootsweb.com/index/intl/NIR/NIR-ANTRIM.html

Armagh
- NIR-Armagh Mailing List
  lists5.rootsweb.com/index/intl/NIR/NIR-ARMAGH.html
- NIR-Armagh-City Mailing List
  lists5.rootsweb.com/index/intl/NIR/NIR-ARMAGH-CITY.html

Carlow
- IRL-CARLOW Mailing List
  lists5.rootsweb.com/index/intl/IRL/IRL-CARLOW.html

Cavan
- IRL-CAVAN Mailing List
  lists5.rootsweb.com/index/intl/IRL/IRL-CAVAN.html

Clare
- IRL-CLARE Mailing List
  lists5.rootsweb.com/index/intl/IRL/IRL-CLARE.html

Cork
- County Cork Mailing List
  lists5.rootsweb.com/index/intl/IRL/CountyCork.html
- IRL-CORK Mailing List
  lists5.rootsweb.com/index/intl/IRL/IRL-CORK.html
- IRL-CORK-CITY Mailing List
  lists5.rootsweb.com/index/intl/IRL/IRL-CORK-CITY.html
- Beara Mailing List
  lists5.rootsweb.com/index/intl/IRL/Beara.html
  Covers the Berehaven Peninsula, Co's Cork and Kerry

Donegal
- Donegal Mailing List
  www.mindspring.com/~dickod/donegal/maillist.html
- IRL-DONEGAL Mailing List
  lists5.rootsweb.com/index/intl/IRL/IRL-DONEGAL.html
- IRL-CO-DONEGAL Mailing List
  lists5.rootsweb.com/index/intl/IRL/IRL-CO-DONEGAL.html
- Donegaleire Mailing List
  lists5.rootsweb.com/index/intl/IRL/DONEGALEIRE.html
- IRL-ARRANMORE Mailing List
  lists5.rootsweb.com/index/intl/IRL/IRL-ARRANMORE.html

Down
- NIR-DOWN Mailing List
  lists5.rootsweb.com/index/intl/NIR/NIR-DOWN.html

Dublin
- IRL-DUBLIN Mailing List
  lists5.rootsweb.com/index/intl/IRL/IRL-DUBLIN.html

- IRL-DUBLIN-CITY Mailing List
  lists5.rootsweb.com/index/intl/IRL/IRL-DUBLIN-CITY.html

Fermanagh

- Fermanagh Mailing List
  lists5.rootsweb.com/index/intl/NIR/FERMANAGH.html

- IRL-Fermanagh
  lists5.rootsweb.com/index/intl/NIR/IRL-FERMANAGH.html

Galway

- IRL-GALWAY Mailing List
  lists5.rootsweb.com/index/intl/IRL/IRL-GALWAY.html

- IRL-ARAN-ISLANDS Mailing List
  lists5.rootsweb.com/index/intl/IRL/IRL-ARAN-ISLANDS.html

- LETTERMULLEN-GALWAY Mailing List
  lists5.rootsweb.com/index/intl/IRL/LETTERMULLEN-GALWAY.html

- IRL-GALWAY-WOODFORD Mailing List
  lists5.rootsweb.com/index/intl/IRL/IRL-GALWAY-WOODFORD.html

Kerry

- IRL-KERRY Mailing List
  lists5.rootsweb.com/index/intl/IRL/IRL-KERRY.html

See also Cork

Kildare

- IRL-CO-KILDARE Mailing Lists
  lists5.rootsweb.com/index/intl/IRL/IRL-CO-KILDARE.html

- IRL-KILDARE Mailing List
  lists5.rootsweb.com/index/intl/IRL/IRL-KILDARE.html

Kilkenny

- IRL-KILKENNY Mailing List
  lists5.rootsweb.com/index/intl/IRL/IRL-KILKENNY.html

- KILKENNY Mailing List
  lists5.rootsweb.com/index/intl/IRL/KILKENNY.html

Laois

- IRL-LAOIS Mailing List
  lists5.rootsweb.com/index/int/IRL/IRL-LAOIS.html

- IRL-LEIX Mailing List
  lists5.rootsweb.com/index/intl/IRL/IRL-LEIX.html

Leitrim

- IRL-LEITRIM Mailing List
  lists5.rootsweb.com/index/intl/IRL/IRL-LEITRIM.html

Limerick

- IRL-LIMERICK Mailing List
  lists5.rootsweb.com/index/intl/IRL/IRL-LIMERICK.html

Londonderry

- NIR-Derry Mailing List
  lists5.rootsweb.com/index/intl/NIR/NIR-DERRY.html

Longford

- IRL-LONGFORD Mailing List
  lists5.rootsweb.com/index/intl/IRL/IRL-LONGFORD.html

Louth

- IRL-LOUTH Mailing List
  lists5.rootsweb.com/index/intl/IRL/IRL-LOUTH.html

Mayo

- IRL-MAYO Mailing List
  lists5.rootsweb.com/index/intl/IRL/IRL-MAYO.html

- MAYO Mailing List
  lists5.rootsweb.com/index/intl/IRL/MAYO.html

- IRL-MAYO-BOHOLA Mailing List
  lists5.rootsweb.com/index/intl/IRL/IRL-MAYO-BOHOLA.html
- IRL-MAYO-CLAREMORRIS Mailing List
  lists5.rootsweb.com/index/intl/IRL/IRL-MAYO-CLAREMORRIS.html
- IRL-MAYO-KILTIMAGH Mailing List
  lists5.rootsweb.com/index/intl/IRL/IRL-MAYO-KILTIMAGH.html
- IRL-MAYO-KINAFFE-SWINFORD Mailing List
  lists5.rootsweb.com/index/intl/IRL/IRL-MAYO-KINAFFE-SWINFORD.html
- IRL-LOUISBURGH mailing list
  lists5.rootsweb.com/index/intl/IRL/IRL-LOUISBURGH.html

In Co. Mayo

Meath

- IRL-MEATH Mailing List
  lists5.rootsweb.com/index/intl/IRL/IRL-MEATH.html

Monaghan

- IRL-MONAGHAN Mailing List
  lists5.rootsweb.com/index/intl/IRL/IRL-MONAGHAN.html

Munster

- IRL-MUNSTER Mailing List
  lists5.rootsweb.com/index/intl/IRL/IRL-MUNSTER.html

Offaly

- IRL-OFFALY Mailing List
  lists5.rootsweb.com/index/intl/IRL/IRL-OFFALY.html

Roscommon

- IRL-ROSCOMMON Mailing List
  lists5.rootsweb.com/index/intl/IRL/IRL-ROSCOMMON.html
- Roscommon Mailing List
  lists5.rootsweb.com/index/intl/IRL/ROSCOMMON.html

Sligo

- IRL-SLIGO Mailing List
  lists5.rootsweb.com/index/intl/IRL/IRL-SLIGO.html
- IRL-BALLYKILCLINE Mailing Lists
  lists5.rootsweb.com/index/intl/IRL/IRL-BALLYKILCLINE.html

Tipperary

- Co. Tipperary Mailing List
  lists5.rootsweb.com/index/intl/IRL/CoTipperary.html
- IRL-TIPPERARY Mailing List
  lists5.rootsweb.com/index/intl/IRL/IRL-TIPPERARY.html

Tyrone

- Co. Tyrone, Ireland, Mailing List
  lists5.rootsweb.com/index/intl/NIR/CoTyroneIreland.html
- IRL-TYRONE Mailing List
  lists5.rootsweb.com/index/intl/NIR/IRL-TYRONE.html
- NIR-Tyrone Mailing List
  lists5.rootsweb.com/index/intl/NIR/NIR-TYRONE.html

Waterford

- IRL-WATERFORD Mailing List
  lists5.rootsweb.com/index/intl/IRL/IRL-WATERFORD.html
- Waterford Mailing List
  lists5.rootsweb.com/index/intl/IRL/WATERFORD.html

Westmeath

- IRL-WESTMEATH Mailing List
  lists5.rootsweb.com/index/intl/IRL/IRL-WESTMEATH.html

Wexford

- IRL-WEXFORD Mailing List
  lists5.rootsweb.com/index/intl/IRL/IRL-WEXFORD.html

- Wexford Mailing List
  lists5.rootsweb.com/index/intl/IRL/WEXFORD.html

Wicklow
- IRL-WICKLOW Mailing List
  lists5.rootsweb.com/index/intl/IRL/IRL-WICKLOW.html

6. Message/Query Boards

A number of websites offer you the opportunity to post messages / queries on the site itself. For a listing of such sites visit:

- Queries and Message Boards
  www.CyndisList.com/queries.htm

See also:
- Virtual Irish Community
  www.vic.ie

Includes Irish roots bulletin boards for each Irish county, not otherwise listed here

- Ireland Visitor Centre (Genweb Project)
  egi.rootsweb.com/~genbbs/index/ireland.htm

Extensive list of bulletin boards - queries, bibles, biographies, deeds, obits, pensions, wills - by county

General Message Boards

- Celtic Origins Message Board
  www.irelandbets.com/irish/message

- General Ireland Queries
  genconnect.rootsweb.com/gc/Ireland/General

- Ireland Genealogy Forum
  genforum.genealogy.com/ireland/

- Irish Emigrant Message Board
  www.theirishemigrant.com/Board/default.asp

- Irish Ancestral Pages
  communities.msn.com/IrishAncestralPages

- Scottish and Irish Genealogy Forum
  pub30.bravenet.com/forum/showasp?usernum=2518170574
- Ireland born Adoptees
  www.bulletinboards.com/view.cfm?comcode=Irish
- Irish Genealogy
  www.myirishancestry.com
  Click on 'message board and forum'
- Irish Genealogy Query Board
  www.io.com/~abrieal/Irishgen/Queryboard/guestbook.html
- Local Names Ireland
  names.local.ie/
  Bulletin board for surnames

Provincial Boards

Connaught
- Province Connaught Ireland Queries
  genconnect.rootsweb.com/gc/Ireland/Connaught

Leinster
- Leinster Province of Ireland Queries
  genconnect.rootsweb.com/gc/Ireland/Leinster

Munster
- Province Munster Ireland Queries
  genconnect.rootsweb.com/gc/Ireland/Munster

Ulster/Northern Ireland
- North Ireland Query Board
  genconnect.rootsweb.com/gc/NorthIreland/General

County Boards

Antrim
- Antrim Ireland Genealogy Forum
  genforum.genealogy.com/ireland/Antrim/
- County Antrim Ireland Queries
  genconnect.rootsweb.com/gc/Ireland/Antrim
- Belfast County, Ireland, Genealogy Forum
  genforum.genealogy.com/ireland/Belfast

Armagh
- Armagh Ireland Queries
  genconnect.rootsweb.com/gc/Ireland/Armagh

Carlow
- Carlow Ireland Genealogy Forum
  genforum.genealogy.com/ireland/Carlow/
- Carlow Ireland Queries
  genconnect.rootsweb.com/gc/Ireland/Carlow

Cavan
- Cavan, Ireland, Genealogy Forum
  genforum.genealogy.com/ireland/Cavan/
- Cavan Ireland Queries
  genconnect.rootsweb.com/gc/Ireland/Cavan

Clare
- Clare, Ireland, Genealogy Forum
  genforum.genealogy.com.ireland/Clare/
- Clare Ireland Queries
  genconnect.rootsweb.com/gc/Ireland/Clare

Cork
- Cork, Ireland, Genealogy Forum
  genforum.genealogy.com.ireland/Cork/
- County Cork, Ireland
  genconnect.rootsweb.com/gc/Ireland/Cork

Donegal

- Donegal, Ireland Connection Boards
  freepages.genealogy.rootsweb.com/~donegaleire/Donconnect.html
  List of bulletin boards, *etc.*

- Co. Donegal Queries
  genconnect.rootsweb.com/gc/Ireland/Donegal

- Donegal, Ireland Genealogy Forum
  genforum.genealogy.com/ireland/donegal/

- Carndonagh/Inishowen Message Board
  users2.cgiforme.com/carn/cfmboard.html

Down

- County Down Ireland Queries
  genconnect.rootsweb.com/gc/Ireland/Down

- Down, Ireland Genealogy Forum
  genforum.genealogy.com/ireland/down

Dublin

- Dublin, Ireland Genealogy Forum
  genforum.genealogy.com.ireland/dublin/

- Dublin Ireland Surname Queries
  genconnect.rootsweb.com/gc/Ireland/

Fermanagh

- County Fermanagh Northern Ireland Queries
  genconnect.rootsweb.com/gc/Ireland/Fermanagh

Galway

- Galway County Ireland Queries
  genconnect.rootsweb.com/gc/Ireland/Galway
  www.rootsweb.com/~irlgal/index2.html

- Galway, Ireland, Genealogy Forum
  genforum.genealogy.com.ireland/galway/

- Galway, Ireland Queries
  genconnect.rootsweb.com/gc/Eire/Galway

Kerry

- County Kerry, Eire, Query Forum
  genconnect.rootsweb.com/gc/Eire/Kerry

- County Kerry Message Board
  genconnect.rootsweb.com/gc/Ireland/Kerry

- Kerry Ireland Genealogy Forum
  genforum.genealogy.com/ireland/Kerry/

- Kildare, Ireland, Genealogy Forum
  genforum.genealogy.com/ireland/Kildare/

Kildare

- Kildare Ireland Queries
  genconnect.rootsweb.com/gc/Ireland/Kildare

Kilkenny

- Kilkenny, Ireland, Genealogy Forum
  genforum.genealogy.com/ireland/kilkenny/

- Region of Kilkenny Ireland Query Forum
  genconnect.rootsweb.com/gc/Ireland/Kilkenny

Laois

- County Laois Ireland Queries
  genconnect.rootsweb.com/gc/Ireland/Laois

- Laois, Ireland, Genealogy Forum
  genforum.genealogy.com/ireland/laois

Leitrim

- County Leitrim, Ireland
  www.eskimo.com/~chance/ireland/leitrim/queries.html

- County Leitrim Ireland Queries
  genconnect.rootsweb.com/gc/Ireland/Leitrim

- Leitrim, Ireland, Genealogy Forum
  genforum.genealogy.com/ireland/Leitrim

- The Leitrim-Roscommon Genealogy Bulletin Board
  www.leitrim-roscommon.com/lrboard/

Limerick

- Limerick, Ireland, Genealogy Forum
  genforum.genealogy.com.ireland/limerick/

- Limerick, Ireland Query Forum
  genconnect.rootsweb.com/gc/Ireland/Limerick

Londonderry

- Derry, NIR Queries
  genconnect.rootsweb.com/gc/Ireland/Londonderry

- County Londonderry
  www.eskimo.com/~chance/ireland/derry/queries.html

- Londonderry, Ireland, Genealogy Forum
  genforum.genealogy.com/ireland/Londonderry

Longford

- County Longford, Ireland, Query Forum
  genconnect.rootsweb.com/gc/Ireland/Longford

- Longford, Ireland, Genealogy Forum
  genforum.genealogy.com/ireland/Longford/

Louth

- County Louth, Ireland Queries
  genconnect.rootsweb.com/gc/Ireland/Louth

- Louth, Ireland, Genealogy Forum
  genforum.genealogy.com/ireland/Louth/

Mayo

- Mayo, Ireland, Genealogy Forum
  genforum.genealogy.com/ireland/mayo/

- Mayo, Ireland Queries
  genconnect.rootsweb.com/gc/Ireland/Mayo

Meath

- Meath, Ireland, Genealogy Forum
  genforum.genealogy.com/ireland/meath/

- Meath, Ireland Queries
  genconnect.rootsweb.com/gc/Ireland/Meath

Monaghan

- Monaghan, Ireland, Genealogy Forum
  genforum.genealogy.com/ireland/monaghan

- Monaghan, Ireland Queries
  genconnect.rootsweb.com/gc/Ireland/Monagahan

Offaly

- Offaly, Ireland Queries
  genconnect.rootsweb.com/gc/Ireland/Offaly

Roscommon

- County Roscommon, Ireland Research and Queries Board
  genconnect.rootsweb.com/gc/Ireland/Roscommon

- Roscommon, Ireland, Genealogy Forum
  genforum.genealogy.com/ireland/Roscommon/

See also Leitrim

Sligo

- Region of Sligo, Ireland, Query Forum
  genconnect.rootsweb.com/gc/Ireland/Sligo

- Sligo, Ireland, Genealogy Forum
  genforum.genealogy.com/ireland/sligo/

Tipperary

- Tipperary, Ireland, Genealogy Forum
  genforum.genealogy.com/ireland/tipperary/

- Tipperary, Ireland Queries
  genconnect.rootsweb.com/gc/Ireland/Tipperary

Tyrone

- County Tyrone, Ireland Queries
  genconnect.rootsweb.com/gc/Ireland/Tyrone

- County Tyrone Query
  www.rootsweb.com/~nirtyr3/Queries.htm

- Tyrone, Ireland, Genealogy Forum
  genforum.genealogy.com/ireland/Tyrone/

Waterford

- Knowhoe Noticeboard for Waterford
  www.knowhoe.co.uk/board/kb490/

- Waterford County Ireland Queries
  genconnect.rootsweb.com/gc/Ireland/Waterford

- Waterford County Ireland Queries
  genconnect.rootsweb.com/gc/Ireland/Waterford

- Waterford, Ireland, Genealogy Forum
  genforum.genealogy.com/ireland/waterford

Westmeath

- Westmeath, Ireland, Genealogy Forum
  genforum.genealogy.com/ireland/westmeath/

- Westmeath, Ireland Queries
  genconnect.rootsweb.com/gc/Ireland/Westmeath

Wexford

- Wexford, Ireland, Genealogy Forum
  genforum.genealogy.com/ireland/wexford/

- Wexford, Ireland Queries
  genconnect.rootsweb.com/gc/Ireland/Wexford

Wicklow

- County Wicklow, Ireland Research and Queries Board
  genconnect.rootsweb.com/gc/Ireland/Wicklow

- Wicklow, Ireland, Genealogy Forum
  genforum.genealogy.com/ireland/wicklow/

7. County Pages

A great deal of information is to be found on county pages. A number of private individuals have created their own county pages, but four organisations have provided pages for every Irish county. The *Irish Times* sites provide the most useful introductory information, but have few links. *Genuki* concentrates attention on primary historical information, rather than on-going and completed research. *Genweb* has some similar information but also includes query boards for each county, and has more information on current and completed research. *Fianna* sites offer a wide range of general information on resources, with many links. *From Ireland* county sites are relatively new, and include information under standard headings such as 'gravestones', 'journals', 'religious records', 'links', *etc.*

The Province of Ulster
   scripts.ireland.com/ancestor/browse/counties/ulster/

Antrim
- Antrim: From Ireland
  www.from-ireland.net/contents/antrimcont.htm
- County Antrim: Fianna's County Page
  www.rootsweb.com/~fianna/county/antrim.html
- Co. Antrim GenWeb
  www.britishislesgenweb.org/northernireland/antrim/
- Genuki Co. Antrim
  www.genuki.org.uk/big/irl/ANT/
- County Antrim, Ireland
  www.rootsweb.com/~nirant/Antrim/
- Co. Antrim's Web Page
  mcfaul.jumpbusiness.com

Armagh
- Armagh: From Ireland
  www.from-ireland.net/contents/armaghconts.htm
- Co. Armagh Gen Web
  www.rootsweb.com/~nirarm
- County Armagh: Fianna County Page
  www.rootsweb.com/~fianna/county/armagh.html
  Addresses and links
- Genuki Co. Armagh
  www.genuki.org.uk/big/irl/ARM/
- County Armagh: Irish Times
  scripts.ireland.com/ancestor/browse/counties/ulster/index_ar.htm

Carlow
- Carlow: From Ireland
  www.from-ireland.net/contents/carlcont.htm
- County Carlow Gen Web
  www.rootsweb.com/~irlcar/
- Genuki Co. Carlow
  www.genuki.org.uk/big/irl/CAR/
- County Carlow: Irish Times
  scripts.ireland.com/ancestor/browse/counties/leinster/index_ca.htm

Cavan
- Cavan: From Ireland
  www.from-ireland.net/contents/cavancont.htm

- Co. Cavan Gen Web
  www.irelandgenweb.com/cavan.html
- Genuki Co. Cavan
  www.genuki.org/big/irl/CAV
- County Cavan. Irish Times
  scripts.ireland.com/ancestor/browse/counties/ulster/index_ca.htm
- Al Beagan's Genealogy Notes of Co. Cavan
  members.tripod.com/~Al_Beagan/tcavan.htm
  Includes many notes on parishes.

Clare

- Clare: From Ireland
  www.from-ireland.net/contents/clareconts.htm
- County Clare: Fianna County Page
  www.rootsweb.com/~fianna/county/clare.html
- County Clare Gen Web
  www.rootsweb.com/~irlcla2/
- Genuki Co. Clare
  home.pacbell.net/nymets11/genuki/CLA/
- County Clare, Ireland
  www.connorsgenealogy.com/clare
- County Clare: Irish Times
  scripts.ireland.com/ancestor/browse/counties/munster/index_cl.htm

See also Limerick

Cork

- County Cork: Fianna County Page
  www.rootsweb.com/~fianna/county/cork.html
- County Cork Gen Web
  www.rootsweb.com/~irlcor
- Genuki Co. Cork
  www.genuki.org.uk/big/irl/COR/
- County Cork: Irish Times
  scripts.ireland.com/ancestor/browse/counties/munster/index_co.htm
- Ginni Swanton's Web Site
  www.ginnisw.com/
  Includes transcripts and indexes etc. of many sources for Co. Cork

Donegal

- County Donegal: Fianna County Page
  www.rootsweb.com/~fianna/county/donegal.htm
- Co. Donegal Gen Web
  www.rootsweb.com/~irldon
- Donegal. From Ireland
  www.from-ireland.net/contents/donegalconts.htm
- Genuki Co. Donegal
  www.genuki.org.uk/big/irl/DON/
- County Donegal: Irish Times
  scripts.ireland.com/ancestor/browse/counties/ulster/index_do.htm
- Donegal, Ireland
  freepages.genealogy.rootsweb.com/~donegaleire/Doncontent.html
- S. W. Donegal Irish Genealogy & our Irish Heritage
  www.radiks.net/~keving/Donegal/DonegalGen.html
  County page; includes much bibliographic information.

Down

- Down: From Ireland
  www.from-ireland.net/contents/downconts.htm
- County Down: Fianna County Page
  www.rootsweb.com/~fianna/county/down.html

- Co. Down Gen Web
  www.rootsweb.com/~nirdow/
- Genuki Co. Down
  www.genuki.org.uk/big/irl/DOW/
- County Down: Irish Times
  scripts.ireland.com/ancestor/browse/counties/ulster/index__dn.htm
- The Down, Ireland, Genealogy Web Site
  www.caora.net

Searchable databases of the Flax Grants (1796), Tithe Record (1820-1830's), Griffiths Valuation (1863), and Census summaries (1901); also message board, chat room, etc.

Dublin

- Dublin: From Ireland
  www.from-ireland.net/contents/dublincontents.htm
- County Dublin: Fianna County Page
  www.rootsweb.com/~fianna/county/dublin.html
- Co. Dublin Gen Web
  www.rootsweb.com/~irldub.
- Genuki Co. Dublin
  www.genuki.org.uk/big/irl/DUB/
- County Dublin: Irish Times
  scripts.ireland.com/ancestor/browse/counties/leinster/index__du.htm

Fermanagh

- Fermanagh: From Ireland
  www.from-ireland.net/contents/fermanconts.htm
- County Fermanagh: Fianna County Page
  www.rootsweb.com/~fianna/county/fermanagh.html
- Co. Fermanagh
  www.rootsweb.com/~nirfer/
- Genuki Co. Fermanagh
  www.genuki.org.uk/big/irl/FER/
- County Fermanagh: Irish Times
  scripts.ireland.com/ancestor/browse/counties/ulster/index__fe.htm
- Fermanagh Gold
  www.fermanagh.org.uk

Galway

- Galway: From Ireland
  www.from-ireland.net/contents/galwayconts.htm
- County Galway: Fianna County Page
  www.rootsweb.com/~fianna/county/galway.html
- Co. Galway Gen Web
  www.rootsweb.com/~irlgal/Galway.html
- Genuki Co. Galway
  www.genuki.org.uk/big/irl/GAL/
- County Galway: Irish Times
  scripts.ireland.com/ancestor/browse/counties/connacht/index__ga.htm

Kerry

- Kerry. From Ireland
  www.from-ireland.net/contents/kerrycontents.htm
- County Kerry: Fianna County Page
  www.rootsweb.com/~fianna/county/kerry.html
- Co. Kerry Gen Web
  www.rootsweb.com/~irlker
- Genuki Co. Kerry
  www.genuki.org.uk/big/irl/KER/
- County Kerry: Irish Times
  scripts.ireland.com/ancestor/browse/counties/munster/index__ke.htm

- Finding your Ancestors in Kerry
  www.rootsweb.com/~irlker/find.htm
  Introduction

- A Dingle, Co. Kerry, Ireland Genealogical Helper
  members.aol.com/waterlilys/

See also Clare

Kildare

- County Kildare: Fianna County Page
  www.rootsweb.com/~fianna/county/kildare.htm

- Co. Kildare Gen Web
  www.rootsweb.com/~irlkid

- Genuki Co. Kildare
  www.genuki.org.uk/big/irl/KIL/

- County Kildare: Irish Times
  scripts.ireland.com/ancestry/browse/counties/leinster/index_ke.htm

- Kildare: From Ireland
  www.from-ireland.net/contents/kilcont.htm

Kilkenny

- County Kilkenny: Fianna County Page
  www.rootsweb.com/~fianna/county/kilkenny.html

- Co. Kilkenny Gen Web
  www.rootsweb.com/~irlkik

- Genuki Co. Kilkenny
  www.genuki.org.uk/big/irl/KIK/

- County Kilkenny: Irish Times
  scripts.ireland.com/ancestor/browse/counties/leinster/index_ki.htm

- Kilkenny. From Ireland
  www.from-ireland.net/contents/kilkenconts.htm

Laois

- County Laois (Queen's, Leix)
  www.rootsweb.com/~fianna/county/laois.html

- Laois (Queen's County) Gen Web
  www.rootsweb.com/~irllao

- Genuki Co. Laois (Queen's)
  www.genuki.org.uk/big/irl/LEX

- County Laois: Irish Times
  scripts.ireland.com/ancestor/browse/counties/leinster/index_la.htm

- Laois (Leix, Queen's County): From Ireland
  www.from-ireland.net/contents/laoisconts.htm

Leitrim

- Leitrim: From Ireland
  www.fromireland.net/contents/leitrimconts.htm

- County Leitrim: Fianna County Page
  www.rootsweb.com/~fianna/county/leitrim.html

- Co. Leitrim Gen Web
  www.irelandgenweb.com/~leitrim

- Genuki Co. Leitrim
  www.genuki.org.uk/big/irl/LET

- County Leitrim: Irish Times
  scripts.ireland.com/ancestor/browse/counties/connacht/index_le.htm

- Genealogy Pages for County Leitrim and County (London)derry
  www.eskimo.com/~chance/ireland

- Leitrim-Roscommon Genealogy Web Site
  www.leitrim-roscommon.com/

Limerick

- County Limerick, Ireland
  www.connorsgenealogy.com/LIM/index.htm

- County Limerick: Fianna County Page
  www.rootsweb.com/~fianna/county/limerick.html

- Co. Limerick Gen Web
  www.geocities.com/Athens/Parthenon/6108/limerick.htm

- Genuki Co. Limerick
  home.pacbell.net/nymets11/genuki/LIM/

- County Limerick: Irish Times
  scripts.ireland.com/ancestor/browse/counties/munster/index__li.htm

- County Limerick Genealogy
  www.geocities.com/jackreidy/limerick.htm

- Limerick: From Ireland
  www.from-ireland.net/contents/limerickconts.htm

- Limerick Roots
  www.limerickroots.ireland.org

- McNamara & McCarthy
  home.att.net/~wexlababe
  Many pages relating to Limerick Clare, and Kerry

Londonderry

- Londonderry (Derry): From Ireland
  www.from-ireland.net/contents/londonderryconts.htm

- County Londonderry: Fianna County Page
  www.rootsweb.com/~fianna/county/derry.html

- Co. Londonderry Gen Web
  www.rootsweb.com/~nirldy

- Genuki Co. Londonderry
  www.users.qwest.net/~dhepburn/genuki

- County Derry: Irish Times
  scripts.ireland.com/ancestor/browse/counties/ulster/index__de.htm

See also Leitrim

Longford

- County Longford: Fianna County Page
  www.rootsweb.com/~fianna/county/longford.html

- Co. Longford Gen Web
  www.rootsweb.com/~irllog

- Genuki Co. Longford
  www.skylinc.net/~lasmith/genuki/LOG/

- Longford: From Ireland
  www.from-ireland.net/contents/longforconts.htm

- Longford Genealogy
  longford.local.ie/genealogy

- Edgeworthstown Parish Scrapbook
  bally.fortunecity.com/coalbrook/7/
  Includes various lists, e.g. famine victims 1847

Louth

- County Louth: Fianna's County Page
  www.rootsweb.com/~fianna/county/louth.html

- Co. Louth Gen Web
  www.rootsweb.com/~irllex2/

- Genuki Co. Louth
  www.genuki.org.uk/big/irl/LOU

- Louth: From Ireland
  www.from-ireland.net/louthcontents.htm

Mayo

- County Mayo: Fianna County Page
  www.rootsweb.com/~fianna/county/mayo.html
- Co. Mayo Gen Web
  www.rootsweb.com/~irlmay/
- County Mayo, Ireland
  www.connorsgenealogy.com/mayo/
  Little information at date of publication, but the site is 'under construction'
- Genuki Co. Mayo
  www.genuki.org.uk/big/irl/MAY/
- County Mayo: Irish Times
  scripts.ireland.com/ancestor/browse/counties/connacht/index_ma.htm
- Co. Mayo, Ireland, Genealogy
  www.geocities.com/Heartland/Acres/4031/mayo.html
- Mayo: From Ireland
  www.from-ireland.net/contents/mayoconts.htm

Meath

- County Meath Fianna County Page
  www.rootsweb.com/~fianna/county/meath.html
- Co. Meath Gen Web
  community-2.webtv.net/shamrockroots/meath/
- Genuki Co. Meath
  www.genuki.org.uk/big/irl/MEA
- Co. Meath: Irish Times
  scripts.ireland.com/ancestor/browse/counties/leinster/index_me.htm
- Meath: From Ireland
  www.from-ireland.net/contents/meathconts.htm

See also Leitrim

Monaghan

- County Monaghan: Fianna's County Page
  www.rootsweb.com/~fianna/county/monaghan.html
- Co. Monaghan Genealogy
  www.rootsweb.com/~irlmog2/
- Genuki Co. Monaghan
  www.genuki.org.uk/big/irl/MOG/
- County Monaghan: Irish Times
  scripts.ireland.com/ancestor/browse/counties/ulster/index_mo.htm
- Monaghan: From Ireland
  www.from-ireland.net/contents/monaghanconts.htm
- Monaghan: the County
  www.exis.net/ahd/monaghan/default.htm

Offaly

- County Offaly (King's): Fianna County Page
  www.rootsweb.com/~fianna/county/offaly.html
- Co. Offaly (King's County) Gen Web
  www.irelandgenweb.com/offaly.html
- Genuki Co. Offaly (King's Co.)
  www.genuki.org.uk/big/irl/OFF/
- County Offaly: Irish Times
  scripts.ireland.com/ancestor/browse/counties/leinster/index_of.htm
- Offaly (King's County)
  www.from-ireland.net/contents/offalyconts.htm

Roscommon

- County Roscommon: Fianna County Page
  www.rootsweb.com/~fianna/county/roscommon.html

- Co. Roscommon Gen Web
  www.rootsweb.com/~irlrosco/
- Genuki Co. Roscommon
  www.genuki.org.uk/big/irl/ROS
- County Roscommon: Irish Times
  scripts.ireland.com/ancestor/browse/counties/connacht/index_ro.htm
- Roscommon: From Ireland
  www.from-ireland.net/contents/roscommconts.htm

Sligo
- County Sligo: Fianna County Page
  www.rootsweb.com/~fianna/county/sligo.html
- Co. Sligo Gen Web
  www.rootsweb.com/~irlsli
- Genuki Co. Sligo
  www.genuki.org.uk/big/irl/SLI
- County Sligo: Irish Times
  scripts.ireland.com/ancestor/browse/counties/connaught/index_sl.html
- Sligo: From Ireland
  www.from-ireland.net/contents/sligoconts

Tipperary
- County Tipperary: Fianna County Page
  www.rootsweb.com/~fianna/county/tipperary.html
- Co. Tipperary Gen Web
  www.rootsweb.com/~irltip/tipperary.htm
- County Tipperary, Ireland
  www.connorsgenealogy.com/tipp/
- Genuki Co. Tipperary
  www.genuki.org.uk/big/irl/TIP
- County Tipperary: Irish Times
  scripts.ireland.com/ancestor/browse/counties/munster/index_ti.htm
- Tipperary: From Ireland
  www.from-ireland.net/contents/tipperconts.htm
- Aid to Genealogical Research in Clogheen & District
  www.amireland/clogheen/clogpage/roots.html
Introduction to parish sources

Tyrone
- County Tyrone: Fianna's County Page
  www.rootsweb.com/~Fianna/county/tyrone.html
- Co. Tyrone Gen Web
  www.rootsweb.com/~nirtyr
- Genuki Co. Tyrone
  www.genuki.org.uk/big/irl/TYR/
- County Tyrone: Irish Times
  scripts.ireland.com/ancestor/browse/counties/ulster/index_ty.htm
- Tyrone: From Ireland
  www.from-ireland.net/contents/tyroneconts.htm

Waterford
- County Waterford: Fianna's County Page
  www.rootsweb.com/~fianna/county/waterford.html
- Co. Waterford Gen Web
  community2-webtv.net/waterfordroots/waterford
- Genuki Co. Waterford
  www.genuki.org.uk/big/irl/WAT
- County Waterford: Irish Times
  scripts.ireland.com/ancestor/browse/counties/munster/index_wa.htm

- Waterford: From Ireland
  www.from-ireland.net/contents/waterfordconts.htm

Westmeath

- County Westmeath: Fianna's County Page
  www.rootsweb.com/~fianna/county/westmeath.html

- Genuki Co. Westmeath
  www.genuki.org.uk/big/URL/WEM

- Westmeath: From Ireland
  www.from-ireland.net/contents/westmeathconts.htm

- Westmeath Gen Web
  www.rootsweb.com/~irlwem

- County Westmeath: Irish Times
  scripts.ireland.com/ancestor/browse/counties/leinster/index__we.htm

Wexford

- County Wexford: Fianna's County Page
  www.rootsweb.com/~fianna/county/wexford.html

- Genuki Co. Wexford
  www.genuki.org.uk/big/irl/WEX/

- Ireland Gen Web: Co. Wexford
  www.rootsweb.com/~irlwex

- County Wexford: Irish Times
  scripts.ireland.com/ancestor/browse/counties/leinster.htm

- Wexford: From Ireland
  www.from-ireland.net/wexfordconts.htm

Wicklow

- County Wicklow: Fianna's County Page
  www.rootsweb.com/~fianna/county/wicklow.html

- Co. Wicklow Gen Web
  members.aol.com/gg4you4170/CountyWicklow/CountyWicklow.htm

- Genuki Co. Wicklow
  www.genuki.org.uk/big/irl/WIC/

- County Wicklow: Irish Times
  scripts.ireland.com/ancestor/browse/counties/leinster/index__wi.html

- Wicklow: From Ireland
  www.from-ireland.net/contents/wicklowconts.htm

8. Surnames

The Internet is an invaluable aid for those who want to make contact with others researching the same surname. There are innumerable lists of surname interests, family web-sites, and surname mailing lists. The two latter categories will not be listed here; they are far too numerous for a book of this length, and many are international in scope rather than purely Irish. Such sites may be found through the gateways listed below.

For general guidance on finding surname information on the web, consult:

- Finding Surname Interests
  www.hawgood.co.uk/finding.htm

General discussion of surnames on the web.

See also:
- Researching Irish Names
  www.rootsweb.com/%7Efianna/surname/

General guidance on using surname lists with many links.

Surname Webpages

Surname web-pages are listed in the following pages:
- A-Z of Ireland Family Surnames Page
  members.tripod.com/~Caryl__Williams/Eirenames-7.html

- Personal Home Pages
  www.CyndisList.com/personal.htm

Good starting point, but with American bias.

- Cyndis List: Surname, Family Association & Family newsletters index
  www.cyndislist.com/surnames.htm

American bias

- Irish Clans & Families
  www.scotlandsclans.com/irclans.htm

Directory of family pages

- Irish Clans, then and now
  pages.prodigy.com/GPGJ41A/clans.htm

Directory of clan and family associations on the internet

- Irish Surname Pages
  www.geocities.com/jackreidy/surnames.htm

- Irish Surnames and Irish Descendants Homepages
  www.geocities.com/Heartland/Meadows/4404/pages.html

Brief gateway

- Links to Irish Names
  www.rootsweb.com/~fianna/name02.html

Surname webpage directory

- Roots Web Surname List
  rsl.rootsweb.com/cgi-bin/rslsql.cgi

International, but with many Irish names

- Surname Helper Home Page
  surhelp.rootsweb.com

Gateway

- Surname Helper Ireland
  surhelp-bin.rootsweb.com/sitelist.pl

Lists (mainly) Irish Gen Web sites

- Surname Websites Located on Rootsweb
  www.rootsweb.com/~websites/surnames/

Probably the most extensive listing of surname sites; American bias

- Surname Resources at Rootsweb
  resources.rootsweb.com/~clusters/surnames/

Interests

The major on-line surname interests listing for Ireland is:
- On-line Irish Names Research Directory
  www.users.on.net/proformat/irlnames.html
Extensive interest lists, by county

See also:
- Genealogical Research Directory
  www.ozemail.com.au/-grdxxx
Webpage for the major published interests listing, available as a book or CD

- Genuki Surname Lists
  www.genuki.org.uk/indexes/SurnamesLists.html
Interests

- The Irish Ancestral Research Association: Members Surname Interests
  tiara.ie/surnames.htm

- Irish Family Surname Interest List
  irishgenealogy.net/surnamef.html

- Irish Millenium Family Register
  familyregister.local.ie
Interests

A variety of databases can be searched at:
- Surname Navigator Ireland
  www.kuijsten.net/navigator/ireland/

County and Local Surname Websites

Antrim
- Co. Antrim Families on the Web
  www.geocities.com/Heartland/Prairie/4592/antlink.html
Directory of web pages

- Co. Antrim's Surname Interest List
  irishgenealogy.net/surname1.html

- The County Antrim Surname Interest List
  website.lineone.net/~british__isles/ANTRIM/antrimsr.htm

Carlow
- County Carlow Surname Registry
  www.rootsweb.com/~irlcar2/registry.htm

Clare
- Clare
  www.users.on.net/proformat/clanames1.html
Surname interests. Continued by **/clanames2.html**

Cork
- Ginni Swanton's Web Site: County Cork Surnames Database
  www.ginnisw.com/Surnames%20Home.htm

Donegal
- County Donegal Surname Researchers
  www.geocities.com/Heartland/Estates/6587/Donresearch.html
Web pages

- Surname Helper, Donegal, Ireland
  surhelp-bin.rootsweb.com/surindx.pl?gc=Ireland/Donegal

- Irish Ancestry.com Donegal & Northwest Ireland Geneological People Locator
  www.irishancestry.com/page4.html
Searches surname web-pages

Down
- Surname Helper, Down, Ireland
  surhelp.bin.rootsweb.com/surindxpl?gc=/Ireland/Down

Dublin
- Surname Helper, Dublin, Ireland
  surhelp-bin.rootsweb.com/surindxpl?gc=Ireland/Dublin

Galway

- County Galway Surname List
  www.labyrinth.net.au/~quibellg/galway.htm

Kerry

- Family Association Websites
  www.rootsweb.com/~irlker/familywebs.html
For Co. Kerry

- Surname Helper, Kerry, Ireland
  surhelp-bin.rootsweb.com/surindxpl?gc=/Ireland/Kerry

Kilkenny

- County Kilkenny Ireland Genealogy: Surnames of Kilkenny
  www.rootsweb.com/ksurname.htm

- County Kilkenny, Ireland, Genealogy: Surnames of Kilkenny
  www.rootsweb.com/~irlkik/ksurname.htm#sons

Gateway to surname pages, coats of arms, etc.

- Surname Helper, County Kilkenny
  surhelp-bin.rootsweb.com/surindx.pl?gc=/Ireland/Kilkenny

Laois

- Surname Helper, Laois, Ireland
  surhelp-bin.rootsweb.com/surindx.pl?gc=Ireland/Laois

Leitrim

- Leitrim-Roscommon Surname Search Page
  www.leitrim-roscommon.com/surname__intro.html

- Surname Helper, Leitrim
  surhelp-bin.rootsweb.com/surindx.pl?gc=/Ireland/Leitrim

Limerick

- Surname Helper, Limerick, Ireland
  surhelp-bin.rootsweb.com/surindx.pl?gc=/Ireland/Limerick

Longford

- Longford Surnames Online
  www.rootsweb.com/~irllog/longford.htm

- Surname Helper, Longford, Ireland
  surhelp-bin.rootsweb.com/surindx.pl?gc=/Ireland/Longford

Mayo

- The County Mayo Surname Interest List
  www.cs.ncl.ac.uk/genuki/SurnamesList/MAY.html

Offaly

- Surnames of County Offaly
  offaly.local.ie/content/28150.shtml/genealogy/surname__origins

Roscommon

- Surname Helper: Roscommon, Ireland surhelp-bin.rootsweb/surindx.pl?gc=/Ireland/Roscommon

See also Leitrim

Tipperary

- County Tipperary Surname Registry
  www.rootsweb.com/~irltip2/
Interests

- Surname Helper, Tipperary, Ireland
  surhelp-bin.rootsweb.com/surindx.pl?gc=/Ireland/Tipperary

- The Tipperary Surnames List
  homepages.ihug.co.nz/~hughw/tip.html

Tyrone

- Tyrone Surname Interests
  www.geocities.com/Heartland/Plains/3576/genuki/

Westmeath
- County Westmeath Surname Registry
  www.rootsweb.com/~irlwem2/registry.htm
Interests

Wexford
- The Wexford Surnames List
  homepages.ihug.co.nz/~hughw/wexford.html

Wicklow
- Surname Helper: Wicklow, Ireland
  surhelp-bin.rootsweb.com/surindx.pf?gc=/Ireland/Wicklow

9. Sources

Information on a wide range of sources is available on the net. This includes much valuable advice; it also includes many sites providing the actual data — although the latter sites are rarely of substantial size. A wide variety of sources have sites devoted to them; these are listed here.

Births, Deaths and Marriages
Introductions
- Civil Registration
  freepages.genealogy.rootsweb.com/~irishancestors/Civil%20Registration.html
- Ginni Swanton's Web Site: Irish Birth Death and Marriage Civil Records
  www.ginnisw.com/irish3.htm
- A guide to the General Register Office of Ireland
  homepage.eircom.net/~seanjmurphy/gro/
- Records of Births, Marriages and Deaths
  www.nationalarchives.ie/birthsmarrdeaths.html
From the National Archives

- State Registration of Births Marriages and Deaths
  scripts.ireland.com/ancestor/browse/records/state
- Irish Civil Records at the General Register Office
  www.genealogy.ie/categories/grorecs/
- Official Records of Births Marriages and Deaths
  www.genealogy.ie/categories/bmd/

- General Register Office (Northern Ireland)
  www.nisra.gov.uk/gro/
- Registrars of Births Deaths and Marriages
  www.nisra.gov.uk/regist.htm
  In Northern Ireland
- How to apply for Birth Death and Marriage Certificates
  www.nisra.gov.uk/gro/apply.htm
- How to Order B/M/D
  www.rootsweb.com/~irllex/howto.htm
- Civil Registration in Ireland: bringing Civil Registration into the 21st Century
  www.dun-laoghaire.com/genealogy/civilreg.htm
  Submission to an official inquiry

Parish Registers

- Parish Registers of the Churches
  freepages.genealogy.rootsweb.com/~irishancestors/Parish%20registers.html
- LDS Film Numbers for Ireland Parish Registers
  www.rootsweb.com/~fianna/county/ldspars.html
- Parish Register Copies in the Library of the Society of Genealogists: Ireland
  www.sog.uk/prc/irl.html
  List

National Databases

- Ireland Births or Baptisms, Deaths & Marriages Exchange
  www.eskimo.com/~chance/misc/
- Irish Family Records
  www.irishfamilyrecords.com/irishrecords/SilverStream/Pages/ircs.html
  Database of Irish births, marriages, census etc., 19th c. Over 2,000,000 records.

- Irish Records Extraction Database
  www.ancestry.com/search/rectype/inddbs/3876.htm
  100,000+ names found in original sources
- Irish Marriages: being an index to the marriages in *Walker's Hibernian Magazine* 1771 to 1812
  home.att.net/~labaths/irish-marriages.htm
- Index to the births marriages and deaths in *Anthologia Hibernica*, 1793-1794
  home.att.net/~cmlabath/anthologia__hibernica.htm
- County CMC Record Project
  www.cmcrp.net/OtherCty
  Christenings, marriages and cemetery records from various counties; also includes extracts from Co. Cavan 1821 census, Co. Wexford 1901 census, and Griffiths Valuation for Co. Wexford, *etc.*

Antrim

- County Antrim Roman Catholic Records
  www.rootsweb.com/~genclass/ireland/antrim/antrimrc.htm
- Island Magee parish marriage records
  www.britishislesgenweb.org/northernireland/antrim/islandmagee.html
  19th c.

Carlow

- Catholic Parish Registers of Fenagh and Myshall, Co. Carlow, Ireland, 1822-1880
  www.rootsweb.com/~irlcar2/fenagh.htm

Clare

- Baptisms, Marriage and other Records: Co. Clare
  www.rootsweb.com/~irlcla/Surname.html
- County Clare CMC Record Project
  www.cmcrp.net/Clare/

- Co. Clare Baptisms: Killard/Kilrush/Kilmurry/Kilmacduane
  freepages.genealogy.rootsweb.com/~msjenkins/records/clarebap.htm
- Deaths in the Liscannor Area 1864-1870
  www.clarelibrary.ie/eolas/coclare/genealogy/deaths_in_the_liscannor_area.htm
  From civil registers

Cork

Cork: From Ireland
  www.from-ireland.net/contents/corkcontents.htm
- County Cork CMC Record Project
  www.cmcrp.net/Cork/
  Christenings, marriages and cemetery records
- Ballyneen District Deaths by surname
  www.ginnisw.com/
  From the civil registers 1864-70
- Births registered in Bandon. Co. Cork 1870
  uk.geocities.com/irishancestralpages/bandon1870b.html
- Ginni Swanton's Web Site: Deaths from Enniskeane Parish Register and Ahiohill Cemetery
  www.ginnisw.com/newpage 1152.htm

Donegal

- Church Records of County Donegal
  donegal.local.ie/content/20616.shtml/genealogy/overview_of_records
  List of registers of the Church of Ireland and the Roman Catholic church, with locations.
- Cloncha Parish births 1669 to 1783: extracts from the parish registers
  freepages.genealogy.rootsweb.com/~donegal/clonchareg.htm
- Union of Strabane Death Index ... Deaths Registered in the District of Raphoe
  freepages.genealogy.rootsweb.com/~donegaleire/Raphdeath.html
  For 1866-7

Down

- Templecraney Cemetery
  www.geocities.com/Athens/rhodes/2830/

Fermanagh

- County Fermanagh Roman Catholic Parish Records
  www.genuki.org.uk/big/irl/FER/RCRecords.html

Galway

- Beagh Parish Catholic Baptisms 1855-1856
  home.att.net/~labaths/births.htm
- Tuam Diocese: Cummer Parish
  pw2.netcom.com/~lgb1/tuamcumm.html
  Marriages 1813-16
- Deaths registered in the District of Loughrea in the Union of Loughrea in the County of Galway
  www.rootsweb.com/~irlgal/index9.html
- Marriages - Parish Register, Catholic Chapelry of Roundstone, parish of Moyrus, Galway 1888-1889
  www.rootsweb.com/~irlgal/index10.html

Kerry

- County Kerry CMC Record Projet
  www.cmcrp.net/Kerry/
- Family History Center Library Catalog Parish Register Film Numbers for County Kerry
  www.rootsweb.com/~irlker/parfilm.html
- On-Line Searchable Database
  www.rootsweb.com/~irlker/addrecords.html
  For Co. Kerry baptisms and marriages
- Baptisms/Birth Records
  www.rootsweb.com/~irlker/birth.html
  Contributed records for Co. Kerry

- Marriage Records, County Kerry, Ireland
  www.rootsweb.com/~irlker/marriage.html

Contributed records

- Burial/Death Records
  www.rootsweb.com/~irlker/burial.html

Contributed records for Co. Kerry

- Brosna R. C. Parish: Diocese of Kerry 1872-1900
  www.limerickroots.ireland.org/OCM3.html

Marriages 1889-1900; Baptisms 1866-1900

- Baptism Locations in Castleisland Roman Catholic Parish
  www.rootsweb.com/~irlker/casparc.html

- Catholic Parish of Keel and Kiltallagh, Co. Kerry:

Marriage Records 1804-1820
  www.shopshamrock.com/genealogy/keel/keel.php3

- Deaths, Lisselton Area
  www.geocities.com/dalyskennelly_2000/deathslisselton.html

Late 20th c

- An Extract of Kerry Marriages in the Barony of Trughanacmy
  www.geocities.com/irishancestralpages/KMmain.html

1874-84

- Kerry Marriages 1877: an extract of Kerry Marriages for the Barony of Troughanacmy
  familytreemaker.genealogy.com/users/o/r/o/Philip-J-Orourke/FILE/0026page.html?Welcome=991647894

Kildare

- Church of Ireland Parish Registers
  Kildare.ie/library/KildareHeritage/page5.html

For Co. Kildare

- Roman Catholic Parish Registers
  Kildare.ie/library/KildareHeritage/page4.html

List for Co. Kildare

Kilkenny

- County Kilkenny, Ireland, Civil Parish Records
  www.rootsweb.com/~irlkik/careclds.htm

List

- St. John's (Maldin Street), Kilkenny
  www.rootsweb.com/~fianna/county/kilkenny/kik-mar3.html#bap

Baptisms 1789-1841; Marriages 1790-1875

- St. Mary's, Kilkenny
  www.rootsweb.com/~fianna/county/kilkenny/kik-mar2.html#bap

Baptisms 1772-1887; marriages 1755-1858.

- St. Patrick's, Kilkenny Marriages 1800's
  www.rootsweb.com/~fianna/county/kilkenny/kik-mar1.html

- Kilmacow Parish Birth Index, County Kilkenny, Ireland (1858 to 1880)
  www.rootsweb.com/~irlkik/records/kilmindx.htm

Limerick

- Civil Parishes of County Limerick
  www.connorsgenealogy.com/LIM/Parishes.html

List with notes on registers

- County Limerick CMC Record Project
  www.cmcrp.net/Limerick

Londonderry

- County Londonderry, Ireland: Roman Catholic Parish Records
  www.eskimo.com/~chance/ireland/derry/rcparish.html

At the Family History Library

Longford

- Church Records
  www.rootsweb.com/~irllog/churchrecs.htm

Indexes of various registers

- County Longford Roman Catholic Parish Records
  personal.nbnet.nb.ca/tmoffatt/RCfilmsLDS.html
  List of LDS films available

Mayo
- County Mayo CMC Record Project
  www.cmcrp.net/Mayo

- County Mayo Roman Catholic Church Records
  www.geocities.com/Heartland/Acres/4031/RCPARISH.HTML
  List of LDS films

- Births and Baptisms in Parishes Westport - Castlebar, Co. Mayo & area
  people.delphi.com/patdeese/BIRTH.HTML
  Updated in: people.delphi.com/patdeese/BALL.HTML

- Marriages in Parishes of Castlebar - Westport - Louisburg, Co. Mayo & area
  people.delphi.com/patdeese/MARR.HTML

- Ballintober Baptisms
  people.delphi.com/patdeese/TOBER.HTML
  1839-97

- Ballintober Marriages
  people.delphi.cm/patdeese/TOB.HTM
  1840-97

- Baptisms in Kilgeever Parish, Co. Mayo
  people.delphi.com/patdeese/KIL.HTML
  Co. Mayo

- Kilgeever Parish Marriage Records
  people.delphi.com/patdeese/KMAR.HTML
  19th c.
  Also /KIL/HTML

- Kiltimagh, Co. Mayo church records: baptisms July 1861 to September 1880
  www.rootsweb.com/~fianna/county/mayo/kiltimaghb.html

- Roundfort Parish, Co. Mayo
  pw2.netcom.com/~lgb1/Ardkell.html
  Baptisms 1899-1916

- Westport area baptisms
  people.delphi.com/patdeese/BAP.HTML
  19th c.

- Westport Parish Marriages 1823 to 1903
  freepages.genealogy.rootsweb.com/~deesegenes/wpt.htm

Monaghan
- Church Registers for County Monaghan
  www.exis.net/ahd/monaghan/churchregisters.htm

- County Monaghan Roman Catholic Records available in the Mormons FHC
  www.exis.net/ahd/monaghan/fhc-rc.htm

Roscommon
- Roscommon: Irish Parish Registers
  www.rootsweb.com/~irlros/irish__parish__registers.htm
  List

- Deaths from the Roscommon Town workhouse
  www.geocities.com/Heartland/Pines/7030/page2.html
  List for mid-late 19th c.

Sligo
- I.G.I. Extracts of Sligo County
  www.rootsweb.com/~irlsli/index2.html

- Castleconnor Parish Records
  www.rootsweb.com/~irlsli/castelconnoropen.html

Tipperary
- County Tipperary CMC Record Project
  www.cmcrp.net/Tipperary
  Christenings, marriage and cemetery records
- Births Registered in Carrick-On-Suir, Tipperary 1871
  www.geocities.com/irishancestralpages/cosbi1871.html
- Clonmel Births 1864-79
  freepages.genealogy.rootsweb.com/~irish/clonmel/cloubirt.htm

Waterford
- County Waterford CMC Record Project
  www.cmcrp.net/Waterford

Westmeath
- Church of Ireland Records: Mullingar 1877-1900
  www.rootsweb.com/~irlwern2/mullingar.htm

Wicklow
- County Wicklow CMC Record Project
  www.cmcrp.net/Wicklow
  Christenings, marriages and cemetery records

Business Records
- Business Records Survey
  www.nationalarchives.ie/cgi-bin/naigenform02?index=Business+Records+Survey

Census
- Census Records
  scripts.ireland.com/ancestor/browse/records/census
  Introduction
- Censuses
  www.rootsweb.com/~fianna/guide/census.html
  Overview of Irish censuses and census substitutes

- Census Returns
  freepages.genealogy.rootsweb.com/~irishancestors/Census%20returns.html
  Introduction
- Census Returns
  www.nationalarchives.ie/censusrtns.html
  From the National Archives
- Irish Census Records
  www.scotlandsclans.com/ircensus.htm
- Irish Census Returns at the National Archives in Dublin
  www.genealogy.ie/categories/cenna/
- Scots and Irish Strays Census Indexes
  rontay.digiweb.com/scot/
- Seventeenth Century Census Substitutes
  scripts.ireland.com/ancestor/browse/records/census/seven.htm
- Eighteenth & Nineteenth Century Census Substitutes
  scripts.ireland.com/ancestor/browse/records/census/eight.htm

Antrim
- 1851 Co. Antrim Census
  mcfaul.jumpbusiness.com

Armagh
- McConville's Irish Genealogy: the first census of the Fews, 1602
  www.mcconville.org/main/genealogy/census1602.html
  The Fews is a barony in Armagh

Clare
- 1901 Census Index: County Clare
  www.connorsgenealogy.com/clare/clarecensuspage.html

See also Limerick

Cork

- Ginni Swanton's Website: 1766 Census Records, Diocese of Cloyne, County Cork
  www.ginnisw.com/1766.htm

- 1911 Census: County Cork
  www.rootsweb.com/~fianna/county/cor1911.html
  List of films at the Family History Library

- 1851 census for Kilcrumper, Kilworth, Leitrim, and Macroney: excerpts
  www.ginnisw.com/1851%20Census%20in%20Excel.htm

Donegal

- Names of Protestant Householders in the year 1766 in the Parish of Leck, Barony of Raphoe, Co.Donegal, Ireland
  freepages.genealogy.rootsweb.com/~donegal/leck1766.htm

- Census Records
  www.geocities.com/Heartland/Lake/6906/census.html
  For Donegal town and its area, Letterkenny, and Stranorlar

- 1901 Census: Crilly, par. Templecarn, Donegal
  freepages.genealogy.rootsweb.com/~msjenkins/records/crilly.htm

- 1901 census for Donegal Town, Inver, Mountcharles & surrounding townlands
  freepages.genealogy.rootsweb.com/~donegal/don1901.html

- 1901 census for Stranorlar Parish
  freepages.genealogy.rootsweb.com/~donegal/stran1901.htm

- 1901 census for Letterkenny
  freepages.genealogy.rootsweb.com/~donegal/Let1901.html

Galway

See Leitrim

Kerry

- 1659 Census, County Kerry, Ireland
  www.rootsweb.com/~irlker/census16a.html
  Pender census

- 1901 census
  www.rootsweb.com/~irlker/census.html
  Co.Kerry; incomplete

- 1901 Census: County Kerry
  www.rootsweb.com/~irlker/census01cp.html

- 1911 Census: County Kerry
  www.rootsweb.com/~irlker/census11.html

- A Census of the Parishes of Prior and Killemlagh, December 1834
  www.rootsweb.com/~irlker/1834text.html

Kildare

- Kildare Heritage & Genealogy Co. 1901 census
  kildare.ie/library/KildareHeritage/Census.htm
  List of computerised 1901 census returns

Leitrim

- Leitrim-Roscommon 1901 Census Home Page
  www.leitrim-roscommon.com/1901census/
  Covers Galway, Leitrim, Mayo, Roscommon, Sligo and Westmeath

Limerick

- 1901 Census of Ireland
  home.att.net/~bristolman/1901__census.htm
  Information from townlands in Co. Limerick and Co. Clare

Londonderry

- 1831 census: Dunboe Parish, Co. Londonderry
  www.rootsweb.com/~nirldy/dunboe/1831cen/1831indx.htm

Longford
- 1901 Census Returns for the Parish of Edgeworthstown
  bally.fortunecity.com/coalbroak/7/Words/Census1.htm

Mayo
- 1901 Census for Gorthbawn, Bellyburke, Killadeer, Cuileen, Co. Mayo
  people.delph.com/patdeese/1901.HTML
- Heads of Household 1901 census for various towns around Westport, Castlebar, Newport, Co. Mayo
  people.delphi.com/patdeese/HEAD.HTML
- 1901 census for County Mayo, Ireland: East Mayo
  www.rootsweb.com/~fianna/county/mayo/emay1910.html
- 1901 Census for the Parish of Burrishoole
  www.geocities.com/Heartland/Park/7461/cens.html

See also Leitrim

Meath
- 1901 County Meath Census
  www.angelfire.com/ak2/ashbourne/townlandlist.html

Roscommon
See Leitrim

Sligo
- Sligo County, Ireland, 1901 Census
  www.rootsweb.com/irlsli/index2.html

See Roscommon

Westmeath
See Roscommon

Church of Ireland
- The Church of Ireland: genealogy and family history
  www.ireland.anglican.org/library/libroots.com

Notes on parish registers and other sources

44

- Church of Ireland Index
  proni.nics.gov.uk/records/private/confiindx.htm

Records at the Public Record Office of Northern Ireland

Louth
- Tullyallen New Church
  www.rootsweb.com/~fianna/county/Louth/loutchu.html

List of subscribers 1898

Confirmation Records
- Ginni Swanton's Web Site Confirmation Records, parishes of Enniskeane, Desertserges and Kinneigh, County Cork
  www.ginnisw.com/confirma1.htm

Deeds
- Registry of Deeds
  scripts.ireland.com/ancestor/browse/records/deeds/

Directories
- Directories
  scripts.ireland.com/ancestor/browse/records/directories

General introduction

- Directories
  www.iol.ie/dublincitylibrary/gadirectories.htm

In Dublin City Library

Clare
- Francis Guy's directory of Munster 1886: Ardnacrusha, Co. Clare
  home.att.net/~labaths/ardna.htm

- Clonlara, Co. Clare, 1886
  home.att.net/~labaths/clonlara.htm

Directory entries

- A general directory of the Kingdom of Ireland 1788: Ennis, County of Clare
  home.att.net/~labaths/1788dire.htm

- Slaters Directory of Ireland 1856: Ennis
  home.att.net/~labaths/1856dire.htm

Cork

- Ginni Swanton's Web Site: Francis Guy's County and City of Cork Directory for the years 1875-1876.
  www.ginnisw.com/

Excludes Cork City

- Henry & Coghlan's General Directory of Cork for 1867
  homepage.eircom.net/~ridgway/hcd.htm

Donegal

- 1824 Pigot's Directory, Donegal
  freepages.genealogy.rootsweb.com/~donegal/1824pigots.htm

- 1846 Slater's Directory, Donegal
  freepages.genealogy.rootsweb.com/~donegal/1846dir.txt

- Notes on Donegal towns: Ballybofey, Ballyshannon, & Donegal Town (from *Slaters Directory* 1857)
  freepages.genealogy.rootsweb.com/~donegal/1857dir.htm

Dublin

- Shaw's Dublin City Directory 1850
  www.loughman.dna.ie/dublin1850

Limerick

- A General Directory of the Kingdom of Ireland 1788: Limerick
  home.att.net/%7Elabaths/lim1788.txt

- Ferrar's Limerick Directory of 1769
  home.att.net/~labaths/lim.htm

City

- Limerick City Directory 1788: an extract from the General directory of the Kingdom of Ireland, 1788
  www.geocities.com/irishancestralpages/limdir1788main.html

- A General Directory of the Kingdom of Ireland 1788: Limerick
  home.att.net/~labaths/lim1788.htm

Longford

- Longford Town Directory 1894
  www.rootsweb.com/~irllog/directory.htm

Mayo

- Slater's Directory 1846
  www.geocities.com/Heartland/Park/7461/unindslat.html

For Burrishoole, Co. Mayo

- Business in Castlebar 1824
  peole.delphi.com/patdeese/CBB.HTML

From a Co. Mayo directory

- Castlebar Directory 1846
  people.delphi.com/patdeese/CAS.HTML

- Westport, Co. Mayo, Ireland Directory 1846
  people.delphi.com/patdeese/WEST.HTML

Incomplete

Ejectment Books

- Surviving Ejectment Books
  www.rootsweb.com/~irlcla/landejectlist.html

For Co. Clare 1816-1914. General description of a source that lists tenants threatened with eviction.

Electoral Registers

- 1926 Register of Electors Killarney
  www.rootsweb.com/~irlker/elkill1.html

Emigrant Savings Bank

- A Users Guide to the Emigrant Bank Records
  www.nypl.org/research/chss/spe/rbk/faids/emigrant.html

The Bank was founded by the Irish Emigrant Society for the Irish in New York

Emigration

There are numerous sites devoted to emigration - especially those giving passenger lists. Sites which deal with just one journey are not listed here as there are far too many. For a general introduction, see:

- Exodus
  www.belfasttelegraph.couk/emigration/

General discussion of Irish emigration

Numerous links are provided at:
- Irish Emigration and Genealogical Research
  wwwvms.utexas.edu/jdana/history/genealogy.html

Gateway site

See also:
- Famine and Emigration Links
  freepages.genealogy.rootsweb.com/~irishancestors/Famine.html

Books are vital resources, and are listed on two sites:
- Emigration
  scripts.ireland.com/ancestor/browse/emigration/index.htm

Bibliographical guide

- Books Related to Irish Migration
  ww3.sympatico.ca/kleonard/Irish.html

Bibliographical notes

The sites of two institutions are important:
- Irish Migration Resource Center
  www.irishmigration.com/

- Immigrant Ships Transcribers Guild
  istg.rootsweb.com/departures/ireland.html

Transcripts of passenger lists from many ships

Other sites with links to passenger lists include:
- Register of Irish Emigrants
  homepage.eircom.net/~seanjmurphy/dir/rie.htm

Submitted entries

- Ireland: Irish Ships Passenger List
  www.scotlandclans.com/irshiplists.htm

Gateway site

- Sites with Genealogical Source Material: Irish Passenger Lists
  freepage.virgin.net/alan.tupman/sites/irish.htm

Includes numerous transcripts

- Irish Passenger Lists
  members.tripod.com/~Data__Mate/irish/irish.htm

Numerous transcripts

- Irish Emigrants
  www.genealogy.org/~ajmorris/ireland/ireemg/ireemg.htm

Transcripts of passenger lists

- Irish Passenger Lists
  members.tripod.com/~Data__Mate/irish/Irish.htm

List of lists

- Passenger Lists arranged by County and Destination
  www.rootsweb.com/~fianna/migrate/shiplists.html

Comprehensive gateway for Irish lists
For emigration to specific places see:

Australia

- The Female Irish (potato famine) orphans: girls to Sydney, Melbourne and Adelaide
  users/bigpond.net.au/convicts/page3.html

Combined passenger lists, 1848-50

Canada

- Irish-Canadian List
  www.bess.tcd.ie/roots/irishcan.htm

- Immigrants to Canada
  ist.uwaterloo.ca/~marj/genealogy/thevoyage.html

General introduction with many links

- Immigration Records
  www.archives.ca/02/02020204_e.html

In the National Archives of Canada

- Grosse-Ile in Quebec: the last resting place for over 6,000 Irish souls
  homepage.eircom.net/~mcmullins/gross-ile.htm

General discussion; no names

- Grosse-Ile and the Irish Memorial: National Historic Site of Canada
  parkscanada.pch.gc.ca/grosseile/

General description; no names

- Irish Famine Migration to New Brunswick 1845-1852
  www.gov.nb.ca/archives/ols/ols.asp

Click under 'Private sector records'

- Prince Edward Island Data Pages: Irish born in PEI before 1846
  homepages.rootsweb.com/~mureid/pei/peirish.html

New Zealand

- List of New Zealand Irish Migrants
  www.geocities.com/nziconnection/immlist.htm

United States

- The Irish in America: Irish Genealogy
  www.pbs.org/wgbh/pages/irish/genealogy.html

Brief guide

- Irish Immigrants Database
  208.249.158.172/ireland/irishpass.htm

To the U.S.A.

- New England Irish Pioneers
  www.ancestry.com/search/rectype/inddbs/1008.htm

17th c.

- Ireland to U.S.A: Cimorelli: Immigration Manifests
  www.cimorelli.com/vbclient/like__irish__b.htm

- Chicago Irish Families 1875-1925
  www.geocities.com/Heartland/Park/7461/chicago.html

- Wilmington, Delaware's Irish Roots
  www.lalley.com

- Irish Immigration into Maryland
  www.clis.umd.edu/~mddlmddl/791/Communities.html/irisha.html#md

Article

- Homepage of New York City's Irish 1800's
  freepages.genealogy.rootsweb.com/~nyirish/research.html

- The Irish in 19th-century Portsmouth, N.H.
  www.fortunecity.com/bally/limerick/123/ports/dir.htm

- Irish Immigrants to Virginia
  ftp.rootsweb.com/pub/usgenweb/va/misc/irishva.txt

List, mid-17th c.

- Wilmington, Delaware's Irish routs
  www.lalley.com

Includes Griffiths valuation,1855, for Annoghdown, Donagh Patrick, Kilcoona, Kilkilvery, Killeany, and Killursa, in Co. Galway; also 1801 census for Cargin, Co Galway

For emigration from specific places see:

Donegal

- Assisted Immigrants from Donegal arriving in Lyttleton, New Zealand, 1855-1874
  freepages.genealogy.rootsweb.com/~donegal/donpass.htm

- Donegal to Australia
  freepages.genealogy.rootsweb.com/~donegal/relief.htm

Emigrant records of the Donegal Relief Fund 1858-62

- Irish to America, departing from Donegal 1848-1851
  freepages.genealogy.rootsweb.com/~donegal/IrishtoAmerica.txt

Kerry

- Lansdowne's Estate in Kenmare Assisted Emigration Plan
  www.rootsweb.com/~irlker/lansdowne.html

- State-Aided Emigration Scheme: Castlemaine
  www.rootsweb.com/~irlker/castlemig.html

Leitrim

- Leitrim Emigration to America / Canada
  www.ultranet/~tdyer/gene/Leitrim__Emmigrants.html

Limerick

- Kilmallock Workhouse Emigration
  home.att.net/~bristolman/kilmallock__workhouse.htm
  1850-51

Roscommon

- Ballykilcline Emigrants
  www.rootsweb.com/~irlros/forced.htm
  1844-52

Sligo

- Ships Sailing from Sligo
  www.rootsweb.com/~irlsli/shipshesli.html

Enclosure Records

- Reports and Returns Relating to Evictions in the Kilrush Union 1849
  www.clarelibrary.ie/eolas/coclare/history/kr__evictions/kr__evictions__enclosures.htm

Numerous pages listing enclosure evictions

Estate Records

Clare

- List of Tenants on Colenel O'Collaghan's Estate, Bodyke, 1890's
  www.clarelibrary.coclare/history/tenants__ocallaghans__estate.htm

Donegal

- Tenants on the Abercorn Donegal Estate, Laggan Area, Co. Donegal, Ireland, 1794
  freepages.genealogy.rootsweb.com/~donegal/abercorn.htm

Kerry

- The Kenmare Papers
  proni.nics.gov.uk/records/private/Kenmare.htm

Estate records of the Kenmare family of Killarney, Co. Kerry; the estate covered much of Co. Kerry, and also various places in Co's. Limerick, Cork, Kilkenny, Laois, Carlow, Tipperary and Clare

Louth

- County Louth: Tenants of Lord Roden, circa 1837
  www.rootsweb.com/~fianna/county/louth/rodn1837.html

Mayo

- 1815 Town of Westport Rent Roll
  people.delphi.com/patdeese/WES.HTML

- Marquis of Sligo rent roll: Old Head estate, Mayo, 1802
  people.delphi.com/patdeese/RENT.HTML

Flax Lists

- Irish Flax Growers List 1796
  www.ancestry.com/search/rectype/inddbs/3732.htm

Database

Donegal

- The 1796 Spinning Wheel Premium Entitlement List
  freepages.genealogy.rootsweb.com/~donegal/flaxlist1.txt

For Co. Donegal. See also /flaxlist2.txt

Kerry

- 1796 Flax Seed Premium Entitlement List: County Kerry
  www.rootsweb.com/~irlker/flax1796.html

Game Licences
- Game Licences
  home.att.net/~labafhs/cl1810g.htm
  List from *Clare journal*, 24 Sept. 1810

Griffiths Valuation
- Griffiths Valuation
  www.bess.tcd.ie/roots/GRIFFITH.HTM
- Griffiths Valuation: a 19th century Irish census substitute
  familytreemaker.genealogy.com/30__griff.html?Welcome=991305839
  Description of an important source
- How to Use Griffiths Valuation / Public Record Office of Northern Ireland
  proni.nics.gov.uk/research/family/griffith.htm
- The Primary Valuation of Tenements
  freepages.rootsweb.com/~irishancestors/Primary%20Valuation.html
- Valuation Office: Genealogy/Archive
  www.valoff.ie/valoff17.htm
  Brief note on Griffiths Valuation

Carlow
- County Carlow genealogy: Griffiths Evaluations (1852): Union of Carlow
  www.rootsweb.com/~irlcar2/valuations.htm

Clare
- Griffiths Valuation 1855
  www.clarelibrary.ie/eolas/coclare/genealogy/griffiths/griffith.htm
  In Co. Clare
- Index to Griffiths Valuation of Ireland for County Clare
  www.geocities.com/Heartland/Valley/5946/griffith.htm
- Townland Database and Griffiths Valuation
  www.rootsweb.com/~irlcla/villages.html
  For Co. Clare

Cork
- Ginni Swanton's Web Site: Griffiths Valuation
  www.ginnisw.com/griffith4.htm
  For various Co. Cork parishes

Donegal
- 1857 Griffiths Valuation of Co. Donegal
  freepages.genealogy.rootsweb.com/~donegal/griffiths.htm
- Beagh Parish Griffiths Valuation in 1850's: Heads of Households
  home.att.net/~labaths/griffith.htm
- 1857 Griffith's Valuation: Derrynacarrow East, or Bellanaboy - Stranasaggart - Commeen, Donegal, Ireland
  www.geocities.com/Heartland/Estates/6587/Grif1857.html
- Griffiths Valuation for Inishkeeragh, no.359; Cloghcor; Fallagowan; Gortgarra
  freepages.genealogy.rootsweb.com/~donegaleire/Dongrifinish.html
- Griffiths Valuation for Templecrone Parish 1857
  freepages.genealogy.rootsweb.com/~donegaleire/Dongrifinish2.html
  Continued in **/Dongrifinish3.html**

Down
- Griffith Valuation: Lawrencetown 1857
  www.lawrencetown.com/griffith.htm

Kerry
- Griffiths Valuations: County Kerry
  www.rootsweb.com/~irlker/griffith.html
  In progress
- Family History Library Film Numbers for (Griffiths) Valuations for Kerry County
  www.rootsweb.com/~irlker/griffilm.html

- Notes from Griffiths Valuation for Brusnagh (Brosna), Castleisland, Currauns, Killeentierna and Nohavel
  www.rootsweb.com/~irlker
- Griffiths Valuation 1851: Civil Parish of Listowel, Barony of Iraghticonnor, County of Kerry
  www.geocities.com/irishancestralpages/gv_listowell_main.html

Leitrim
- Leitrim-Roscommon Griffiths Database
  www.leitrim-roscommon.com/GRIFFITH/

Limerick
- Intro to Griffiths Valuation
  www.geocities.com/jackreidy/grifintr.htm
  For S.W. Co. Limerick

Longford
- Griffiths Valuation (1860+), Union of Ballymahon
  www.rootsweb.com/~irllog/valuations.htm
  Incomplete

Mayo
- Griffith Valuation for Co. Mayo
  people.delphi.com/patdeese/GRIF.HTML
- Online Database: Templemore, Mayo Valuation, 1856-1857
  www.everton.com/FHN/fhn1998/21May98.htm

Roscommon
See Leitrim

Sligo
- Sligo Griffiths Valuation Records
  www.rootsweb.com/~irlsli/griffithsopen.html
- Sligo Griffiths Valuation records
  www.rootsweb.com/~irlsli/index2.html

Wicklow
- Griffiths Valuation April 1854
  www.rootsweb.com/~irlwic/Griff.htm

Hearth Tax
Donegal
- A list of persons who paid Hearth Tax in 1665 in the parish of Clonleigh, Donegal, Ireland
  freepages.genealogy.rootsweb.com/~donegal/clonleigh.htm
- Householders in Culdaff who paid a Hearth Tax in 1665
  freepages.genealogy.rootsweb.com/~donegal/culdaffhearth.htm
- The Hearth Money Roll for the Parish of Donoughmore, Donegal ... in 1665
  freepages.genealogy.rootsweb.com/~donegal/hdonough.htm
  thor.prohosting.com/~hughw/donoughm.txt
- Hearth Money Roll, 1665 for the parish of Leck, in the Barony of Raphoe, Co. Donegal, Ireland
  thor.prohosting.com/~hughw/leck1665.txt
- Hearth Money Roll 1665 for the parish of Leck in the Barony of Raphoe, Co. Donegal
  freepages.genealogy.rootsweb.com/~donegal/leck1665.htm
- 1665 Hearth Money Roll for Lettermacaward
  freepages.genealogy.rootsweb.com/~donegal/letterhr.htm
- Persons who paid Hearth Tax in the parish of Raphoe (including) Convoy, in Co. Donegal, Ireland in the year 1665
  freepages.genealogy.rootsweb.com/~donegal/raphoe.htm
  thor.prohosting.com/~hughw/raphoe.txt
- 1665 hearth money roll for Templecrone
  freepages.genealogy.rootsweb.com/~donegal/templehr.htm

- Persons who paid Hearth Money Tax in the parish of Taughboyne, Barony of Raphoe, Co. Donegal, Ireland, in 1665
  freepages.genealogy.rootsweb.com/taughboy.htm
  thor.prohosting.com/~hughw/taughboy.txt

Tipperary
- 1664 Hearth Money Rolls for the Baronies of Ida and Offa, Co. Tipperary
  freepages.genealogy.rootsweb.com/~irish/Tipperary/1664iffa.htm

Land Records
- Land Records
  scripts.ireland.com/ancestor/browse/records/land

- Names of the Cromwellian Adventurers for land in Ireland
  www.exis.net/ahd/monaghan/advntntrs.htm
  In 1642-6

- Lands Grants in the Barony of Raphoe, County Donegal, 1608
  members.aol.com/dngl1608.html

- Pynnar's Survey, 1618 A.D. of the land grants given in 1608, Barony of Raphoe
  members.aol.com/Manus/dng1618.html

Landowners Census
Armagh
- Landowners in Co. Armagh circa 1870's
  www.rootsweb.com/~nirarm/landowners.html

Clare
- Land Owners in Clare: return of owners of land of one acre and upwardss in County Clare, 1876
  www.clarelibrary.ie/eolas/coclare/genealogy/land__owners__in__clare.htm

Cork
- Land Owners in Ireland 1876: County Cork
  www.ginnisw.com/
  Facsimiles

- Return of Owners of Land ... 1876: Mallow
  www.rootsweb.com/~irlmahs/mloii.htm

Galway
- Landowners in Co. Galway, circa 1870's
  www.rootsweb.com/~irlgal/Landowners.html

Longford
- Landowners of County Longford in the 1870's
  www.rootsweb.com/~irllog/landown.htm

Roscommon
- Landowners of Roscommon County in 1871
  www.rootsweb.com/~irlros/returnof.htm

Sligo
- Land Owners in Co. Sligo, late 1870's
  www.rootsweb.com/~irlsli/landowners.html

Westmeath
- Landowners in Co. Westmeath, circa 1870's
  www.rootsweb.com/~irlwem/Landowners.html

Loyalist Claims
- Claims of 1798 Loyalists
  www.geocities.com/Heartland/Park/7461/claim1798.html
  In Burrishoule, Co. Mayo

Marriage Licence Bonds
Clare
- Killaloe, Co. Clare Marriage License Bonds, 1680-1720 and 1760-1762
  home.att.net/~labfhs/killaloe.htm

Laois

- Church of Ireland Marriage Licences from Diocese of Dublin, 1638-1764
  www.rootsweb.com/~irllex/groom.htm
  For Co. Laois

Longford

- Church of Ireland Marriage Licences from Diocese of Dublin, 1732-1757
  www.rootsweb.com/~irllog/groom.htm
  For Co. Longford

Tipperary

- Church of Ireland Marriage Licences from Diocese of Dublin (Tipperary Names) 1732-1764
  www.rootsweb.com/~irltip2/

Westmeath

- Church of Ireland Marriage Licences from Diocese of Dublin, 1680-1764
  www.rootsweb.com/~irlwem2/groom.htm
  From Westmeath

Monumental Inscriptions

- Cemetery Records Online
  www.interment.net/ireland/
  Directory, with transcriptions of records

- Gravestone Records
  scripts.ireland.com/ancestor/browse/records/graveyard
  Introduction

- Gravestone Transcriptions
  www.from-ireland.net/contents/graves.htm

- Irish Cemetery Records
  www.scotlandsclans.com/ircemeteries.htm
  Links to numerous transcripts of inscriptions, etc.

- Saving Graves Ireland
  www.savinggraves.com/ireland/
  Preservation and restoration of graveyards

Carlow

- Memorials of the Dead, Killerig & Tullow Churchyards
  www.rootsweb.com~irlcar2/memorials.htm

Cavan

- Inscriptions in Killeshandra Old Cemetery
  homepages.iol.ie/~galwill/histtombe.htm

- Knocktemple Old Cemetery Inscriptions, County Cavan, Ireland
  www.ancestry.com/search/rectype/inddbs/4225.htm

Clare

- Monumental Inscriptions from Co. Clare Graveyards
  home.att.net/%Ewexlababe/co__clare__graveyards.htm

Donegal

- Cemeteries of Donegal
  freepages.genealogy.rootsweb.com/~donegaleire/Cemeteries.html

- Monumental Inscriptions
  freepages.genealogy.routsweb.com/~donegal/mis.htm
  General discussion with links to Donegal sites

- The Gravestone Inscriptions, St. Anne's Church of Ireland, Ballyshannon
  freepages.genealogy.rootsweb.com/~donegal/stanne.htm

- Assaroe Abbey Cemetery, Ballyshannon
  freepages.genealogy.rootsweb.com/~donegal/assaroecem.htm

- Finner, Bundoran
  freepages.genealogy.rootsweb.com/~donegal/finner.htm
  Monumental inscriptions

- The Gravestone Inscriptions, Gartan Graveyard
  freepages.genealogy.rootsweb.com/~donegal/gartgrave.htm
- Inscriptions in Killeshandra Old Cemetery
  homepages.iol.ie/histtomb.htm
- Leck Cemetery, Letterkenny, Donegal, Ireland
  freepages.genealogy.rootsweb.com/~donegaleire/Donleck.htm
  Gravestone Inscriptions
- Magheragallon Old Graveyard, Tullaghobegley
  freepages.genealogy.rootsweb.com/~donegal/magheracem.htm

Down

- Templecraney Cemetery
  www.geocities.com/Athens/rhodes.2830/

Galway

- Inscriptions from Shanaglish, Beagh Parish, Galway
  home.att.net/~labaths/cembeagh.htm

Kerry

- Gravestone Inscriptions, Abbeydorney, Co. Kerry
  kerry.local.ie/content/31975.html
- Gravestone Inscriptions, Ardfert, Co. Kerry
  kerry.local.ie/content/30238.shtml
- Brosna Cemetery Inscriptions
  www.geocities.com/bluegumtrees/cemetery.html
- Killorglin Tombstone Inscriptions
  www.rootsweb.com/~irlker/tombkillor.html
- Cemetery Inscriptions: Listowel Area
  www.rootsweb.com/~irlker/tomblist.html

Laois

- Memorials of the Dead: Dysart (Enos) Churchyard
  www.rootsweb.com/~irllex/memorials.htm

- Memorials of the Dead: Killinard Churchyard
  www.rootsweb.com/~irllex/memorials2.htm

Limerick

- Abbreviated Head Stone Inscriptions in Ardagh Cemetery
  home.att.net/~wexlababe/abbreviated_headstone_inscriptions.htm
- Monumental Inscriptions in the Civil Parish of Kilbeheny
  home.att.net/wexlababe/monumental_inscriptions_kilbeheny.htm
- Cemetery Inscriptions, Kilmacow Cemetery, Kilmacow, Kilfinny, Co. Limerick
  jamo8.www5.50megs.com/kilmacow.htm
- Rathkeale Graveyard, Co, Limerick
  home.att.net/%7Elabaths/cemlim.htm

Longford

- Newtownbond Church Graveyard
  www.geocities.com/grymorgan

Mayo

- Extracts from Inscriptions in Westport - Castlebar area
  freepages.genealogy.rootsweb.com/~deesegenes/cem.html
- Ashagower Cemetery
  people.delphi.com/patdeese/AG.HTM
- Burrishoole Cemetery
  www.geocities.com/Heartland/Park/7461/graves.html/
- Kilmovee Stained Glass Windows
  homepage.eircom.net/%7Ekevm/Kilmovee/Kilmovee.htm
  Inscriptions

Roscommon

- Baslic Cemetery
  homepage.eircom.net/%7Ekevm/Baslic_2.htm

Sligo
- Banada Abbey
  homepage.eircom.net/%EKevm/Banada_Abbey/Banada_Abbey.htm
  Monumental inscriptions

- Curry
  homepage.eircom.net/%Ekevm/Curry/Curry_Church.htm
  Monumental Inscriptions

- Grangemoor Burial Ground
  www.rootsweb.com/~irlsk/cemetery1.html

- Roslea Cemetery, Easky
  www.rootsweb.com/~irlsli/cemetery/2a.html
  Inscriptions

- Rosser Point Cemetery
  homepage.circom.net/%7Ekevm/Rosses_Point/intro.htm

- St. Attracta's, Thurlestrane: Stained Glass Windows
  homepage.eircom.net/%7Ekevm/Thurlestrane/thurlestrane.htm
  Inscriptions

Tipperary
- Some Memorials to the Dead: Ardcrony Churchyard
  www.rootsweb.com/~irltip2/

- Some Memorials to the Dead: Killardry Churchyard
  www.rootsweb.com/~irltip2/

Tyrone
- County Tyrone Cemetery Index
  www.rootsweb.com/~nirtyr3/Cemetery/cemetery.html
  Includes inscriptions from various cemeteries

- Killeeshil Chapel
  www.rootsweb.com/~nirtyr3/Cemetery/Killeeshil2.htm

Muster Rolls
Donegal
- The Muster Roll of the County of Donnagall 1630 A.D., as printed in the *Donegal Annual*
  members.aol.com/Manus/dngl1630.html

Londonderry
- County Derry 1631 Muster Roll
  www.rootsweb.com/~fianna/county/derry/ldy-1631.html
- Muster Roll of Ironmongers Estate (circa 1630)
  members.aol.com/Manus.derry1630.html

Newspapers
- Newspapers
  scripts.ireland.com/ancestor/browse/records/news/
- Newspapers
  www.iol.ie/dublincitylibrary/ganewspapers.htm
  In Dublin City Library
- The *Belfast Newsletter* index 1737-1800
  www.ucs.louisiana.edu/~jcg3525/Main.html
- Norman Ross Publishing Inc. Irish Newspapers on 35 mm. silver holide positive film from the British Library's Newspaper Library Colindale
  www.nross.com/newsiri1.htm
  Historic Irish newspapers available for purchase
- Index to Biographical Notices in the *Clare Champion* newspaper 1935-1985
  www.clarelibrary.ie/eolas/coclare/genealogy/champions/champion.htm
- Limerick Chronicle Obituaries 1850
  uk.geocities.com/irishancestralpages/lc1850main.html
- The Newspaper Collection
  ireland.iol.ie/%Etipplibs/Newspapr.htm
  Of Tipperary Libraries

Petitions

- 1916 Petition to split Knocknagoshel from the Diocese of Brosna
  www.rootsweb.com/~irlker/parishpet.html

- Clare Men in Favour of Union of Britain and Ireland 1799
  home.att.net/~labaths/1799cl.htm
  List from the *Ennis Chronicle*

Plea Rolls

- The Medieval Irish Plea Rolls: an introduction
  www.nationalarchives.ie/pleas__1.html

Poll Tax

- County Donegal Surname on the Census, 1659: Poll Money Ordinances
  www.geocities.com/Heartland/Estates/6587/Doncensus.html

Presbyterian Records

- Index to Presbyterian Church Records
  proni.nics.gov.uk/records/private/presindx.htm
  Held by the Public Record Office of Northern Ireland

Roman Catholic Records

- Local Catholic Church History and Genealogy Ireland
  home.att.net/%ELocal__Catholic/Catholic__Ireland.htm
  Includes list of counties with their dioceses, much historical information, and many links

- Catholic Qualification Rolls Index: County Monaghan, c.1778
  www.exis.et/ahd/monaghan/qual-cath.htm
  List of those who took the oath of loyalty

School Records and Registers

- National School Records
  www.nationalarchives.ie/natschs.html
  Details of records in the National Archives

- 1824 Survey of Irish Schools
  www.rootsweb.com/~irlker/schoolsur.html
  General discussion of a source for teachers

Donegal

- Register of the old Killybegs Commons School
  freepages.genealogy.rootsweb.com/~donegal/Killybegsns.htm

- Raphoe Royal School: students names
  freepages.genealogy.rootsweb.com/~donegaleire/Rapschool.html
  In 1849

Down

- The Old School Registers: Lawrencetown Male National School, 1870 to 1898
  www.lawrencetown.com/reg1.htm

- The Old School Registers: Lawrencetown Female National School, 1880 to 1923
  www.lawrencetown.com/reg2.htm

Limerick

- Sacred Heart College 1859-1909
  home.att.net/~J-McCarthy/sacred__heart__college.limerick.htm#pupils1859
  List of pupils of a Limerick School

- Schools and School Teachers: Murroe and Boher, Co. Limerick, 1852-1964
  www.geocities.com/irishancestralpages/murbohlim.html

Meath

- Ashbourne National School Register of Names from 1870 to 1906
  www.angelfire.com/ak2/ashbourne/reginfs1.html

Tithes

- Tithe Composition and Applotment Books
  freepages.genealogy.rootsweb.com/~irishancestors/Tithe%20books.html
  Introduction

- Tithe Applotment Books and Primary Valuation
  www.nationalarchives.ie/titheapplprimvalu.html
  From the National Archives

- The Tithe Defaulters, 1831
  www.ancestordetective.com/ireland.tithe.htm

Cork

- Ginni Swanton's Web Site: Tithe Applotment Records, parish of Desertserges, Diocese of Cork April 1829
  www.ginnisw.com/tithe.htm

Donegal

- Tithe Applotment Books for the Parishes of Killybegs, Upper and Lower
  freepages.genealogy.rootsweb.com/~donegal/killytithe.txt

- Tithe Applotment Book for the parish of Garton
  freepages.genealogy.rootsweb.com/~donegal.gartant.htm

- Templecrone Parish Records for Tithe and Griffiths Valuation
  www.geocities.com/Heartland/Shores/1110.tith-list.htm

- Tithe Applotment Survey 1823-37: County Kerry
  www.rootsweb.com/~irlker/tithe.html
  In progress

- Heads of Household of Ballyferriter Catholic Parish, Barony of Corkaguiny, County Kerry, Ireland, 1827-1852
  www.geocities.com/Athens/Ithaca/7974/Ballyferriter/compilation.htm
  From Tithe applotment books 1827-31, a religious census 1834, and Griffiths Valuation 1851-2.

- Tithe Valuation, Brosna Parish, Co. Kerry, Ireland, c.1820
  www.geocities.com/bluegumtrees/griffiths.html

Limerick

- Tithe Records, 1820's: Killeedy, Co. Limerick
  www.geocities.com/curtingenealogy/titheKilleedy.html

Sligo

- Sligo Tithe Applotment Book
  www.rootsweb.com/~irlsli/index2.html

- Tithe Applotment Book: Parish of Easky
  www.rootsweb.com/~irlsli/tithe1.html
  Continued in /tithe2.html/c.1833

Tipperary

- The Parish of Outeragh, County Tipperary, Ireland
  www.ancestordetective.com/ireland/outeragh.htm
  Based on Tithe Applotment Book, Griffiths Valuation, etc.

Transportation Records

- Transportation Records 1791-1853
  freepages.genealogy.rootsweb.com/~irishancestors/AusT.html

- National Archives of Ireland Transportation Records Database
  www.nationalarchives.ie/search01.html
  Transportation to Australia

- Larry Brennan's Page
  www.rootsweb.com/~irlcla/ClareConvictstoAustralia.html
  Co. Clare convicts transported to Australia

- Genseek: Ratcliffe Convicts 1845
  www.standard.net.au/~jwilliams/rat.htm
  List of Irish convicts who arrived in Tasmania in 1845

Donegal

- National Archives of Ireland: Convicts from Donegal to Australia covering the period 1788 to 1868
  freepages.genealogy.rootsweb.com/~donegal/iconoz.txt
  List

- People Involuntarily Transported to America from Donegal 1737 to 1743
  freepages.genealogy.rootsweb.com/~donegal/involtrans.htm

Louth

- Coun*y Louth. Dundalk Householders 1837
  www.rootsweb.com/~fianna/county/louth/loufree1837.html
  From Valuation Office House Book

Roscommon

- Criminals Deported from Co. Roscommon to Australia, 1836-53
  www.rootsweb.com/~irlros/transported.htm

Vietnam Veterans

- The Irish on the Wall: Irish men and women whose names are on the Vietnam Veterans Memorial (the Wall) in Washington, D.C.
  www.irishonthewall.com

Wills

- Wills
  scripts.ireland.com/ancestor/browse/records/wills
  General introduction

- Wills and Administrations
  www.nationalarchives.ie/willsandadmin.html
  From the National Archives

- Old Ireland wills
  members.tripod.com/~Caryll__Williams/wills.html
  Transcripts of submitted wills. Not many yet, but likely to grow

Cavan

- Wills/Admons: County Cavan: a national listing of resources
  freepages.genealogy.rootsweb.com/~colin/Ireland/CavanWills.htm
  Where to look

Cork

- Index to Irish wills: Dioceses of Cork and Ross
  www.ginnisw.com/

Donegal

- Index of Wills, Diocese of Raphoe 1684-1858
  freepages.genealogy.rootsweb.com/~donegal/wills.htm

Sligo

- Killala and Achonry Diocese Wills, County Sligo
  www.rootsweb.com/%7Eirlsli/willssligohome.html
  List

10. Occupational Records

The occupations of our ancestors generated an immense amount of documentation, much of which is of value to the family historian. An introduction to these sources is provided by:

- Occupational Records
  scripts.ireland.com/ancestor/browse/records/occupation

Clergy
Donegal
- Clergy of Templecrune, Arranmore, Falcarragh, Killult, Raymunterdoney and Tullaghobegley to 1900
  freepages.genealogy.rootsweb.com/~donegal/clergy.htm

Kerry
- List of 'Popish Parish Priests' in Kerry, 1704
  www.rootsweb.com/~irlker/popish.html

Convicts & Prisoners
- Out of the Jails: Irishmen Again Free
  home.att.net/~J-McCarthy/1922__out__of__the__jails.htm
  List of Irish prisoners released in 1922

- 1849 May Convictions
  people.delphi.com/patdeese/CONVICT.HTML
  List of convicts

- Genseek Return of Prisoners found Guilty at Spring Assizes 1845, Neenagh, Co. Tipperary
  www.standard.net.au/~jwilliams/pris45.htm

- Neenagh Gaol: Removal of Convicts
  www.standard.net.au/~jwilliams/tgaol.htm
  List, 1845

Freeholders
- County Louth Freeholders 1822
  www.rootsweb.com/~fianna/county/louth/loufree1822.html
- County Louth Freeholders 1824 (supplementary records)
  www.rootsweb.com/~fianna/county/louth/loufree1824.html

Landowners
- Landowners Map of County Kilkenny, c.1640
  www.rootsweb.com/~irlkik/landomap.htm

Pawnbrokers
- Pawnbrokers in Limerick 1837 & 1877
  home.att.net/~tcdman/limerick__pawnbrokers.htm

Police
- Records of the Royal Irish Constabulary
  www.pro.gov.uk/leaflets/n2161.htm

- Police History.com: Garda Siochana Historical Society - Irish Police History
  www.geocities.com/CapitalHill/7900/

- Royal Ulster Constabulary Museum
  www.ruc.police.uk/main/vm.htm

- Royal Irish Constabulary Service Records
  www.ruc.police.uk/museum/gene.htm

Kerry
- Kerry R.I.C. Record Excerpts for 1848-1852
  www.rootsweb.com/~irlker/ric.html
  Co. Kerry police

Longford
- Award of Pensions
  www.rootsweb.com/~irllog/police.htm
  On disbandment of the Royal Irish Constabulary in Co.Longford, 1919

Soldiers
- Finding and Using Irish Military Records
  www.rootsweb.com/~fianna/guide/military.html
- King James's Irish Army List
  www.irishroots.com/KJames.html
- Jacobite Army 1689
  jamo8.ww5.50megs.com/Jacobite%20Army.html
- Civil War Rosters: Irish Regiments
  www.geocities.com/Area51/Lair/3680/cw/irish.html

Names of soldiers in the U.S. Civil War

- The Irish Pensioners of William III's Huguenot Regiments, 1702
  home.att.net/~cmlabath/huguenotpensioners.htm
- WWI Officers from Co. Kerry
  www.rootsweb.com/~irlker/ww1officer.html
- Cork Battalion 1916
  freepages.genealogy.rootsweb.com/~bwickham/corkbatt.htm
- Irish Officers in the United States Army, 1865-1898
  www.rootsweb.com/~irlker/officers1865.html

11. Miscellaneous Sites

Administrative Areas
- Administrative Areas of the British Isles
  www.genuki.org.uk/big/Regions

Includes pages on the Republic of Ireland, and Northern Ireland

- The Ire Atlas Townland Database
  www.seanruad.com

Database of townlands, parishes, counties, baronies, etc.

- O.S. Parish List
  www.nationalarchives.ie/cgi-bin/naigenform02?index=OS+Parish+List
- Geographical Index Northern Ireland
  proni.nics.gov.uk/geogindx.htm

Locates townlands, parishes, baronies & Poor Law Unions, *etc.*

- Townlands of Donegal, listed by Parish
  www.geocities.com/Heartland/Estates/6587/Dontown.html

List

Adoption
- Irish Adoption Contact Register
  www.adoptionireland.com
- Searching in Ireland
  www.netreach.net/~steed/search.html

For Irish-born adoptees

Anglo-Irish
- Anglo-Irish Families in Kilkenny County (1300)
  www.rootsweb.com/__irlkik/kfamily.htm

Casey Collection
- Casey Collection extracts
  www.rootsweb.com/~irlker/casseyrec.html

For Co. Kerry

- Kerry Records in the Casey Collection
  www.rootsweb.com/~irlker/casey.html

Chapman Codes
- Chapman Codes for Ireland
  www.genuki.org.uk/big/IrelandCodes.GIF

Easter Rising
- Ireland: the Easter Rising 1916
  www.pro.gov.uk/leaflets/ri2065.htm

Famine
- The Great Famine 1845-50. Introduction
  www.nationalarchives.ie/famine.html

Gazetteers
- Ireland Gazetteer and Surname Guide
  www.ancestry.com/search/rectype/inddbs/3856.htm

Heraldry
- Coats of Arms in Ireland and around the world
  homepage.tinet.ie/~donnaweb

- Irish Genealogy & Coats of Arms
  www.ireland-information.com/heraldichall/irishcoatsofarms.htm

- Office of the Chief Herald
  www.nli.ie/fr__offi.htm

- Proto-Heraldry in Early Christian Ireland: the Battle Standards of Gaelic Irich Chieftains
  www2.......smumn.edu/uasal.IRHERALD.html

Clare
- Heraldry and Families of County Clare
  www.clarelibrary.ie/eolas/coclare/genealogy/herald.htm

Homicides
- Homicides from 1848-1870 in County Westmeath
  www.rootsweb.com/~irlwern2/wstmurd.html

Huguenots
- French Huguenot Sources
  freepages.genealogy.rootsweb.com/~irishancestors/Hug.html
Brief introduction

- The Huguenot Society of Great Britain and Ireland
  www.local.ie/content/27567.shtml

- Huguenot Surnames
  www.rootsweb.com/%7Efianna/surname/hug1.html
In Ireland

- Huguenot Surnames
  www.rootsweb.com/~fianna/surname/hug1.html

- 1696-1996. St. Paul's Church, Arlington. The French Church
  ireland.iol.ie/~offaly/stpauls.htm

Jews
- The Jews of Ireland Genealogy Page
  homepage.tinet.ie/~researchers

Journals and Newsletters
- Irish Journals with Genealogical Content
  www.from-ireland.net/journalcontent.htm
Valuable listing

- Archaeological and Historical Journals
  www.xs4all.nl/~tbreen/journals.html
Many of the journals mentioned here have genealogical content

- Irish Chronicles Project
  www.genealogy.org/~ajmorris/ireland/icp/icp.htm
Email journal

- The Irish Link: Family History Magazine
  www.netspace.net.au/~gwenoc/
- Irish Roots Magazine Homepage
  www.iol.ie/~irishrts

Includes useful articles

- O'Lochlainns Irish Family Journal
  www.irishroots.com
- The Cavan Genealogist
  ireland.iol.ie/~kevins//index__geneo.html

Email newsletter

Knights

- Knights Bachelor knighted in Ireland
  www.rootsweb.com/%7Efianna/surname/knights.html

Local History

- Island Ireland directory for Irish Local History
  islandireland.com/Pages/history/local.html

Gateway to Irish local history

Look-Ups

- Books We Own: Ireland & Northern Ireland
  www.rootsweb.com/~bwo/ireland.html
- Genealogy Helplist Ireland
  www.crosswinds.net/~mollynidana/genealogy/helplistireland.htm

Carlow

- County Carlow Lookups
  www.rootsweb.com/~irlcar2/lookup.htm

Clare

- County Clare, County Limerick Lookup Service
  www.connorsgenealogy.com/lookups.html

Lookups offered on various databases

Galway

- Galway County Look-up Page
  www.rootsweb.com/~irlgal/index1.html

Kerry

- County Kerry Lookups
  www.rootsweb.com/~irlker/lookup.html

Kilkenny

- County Kilkenny Lookup Service
  www.rootsweb.com/~irlkik/klookup.htm

Limerick

See Clare

Mayo

- Mayo County Lookups
  www.geocities.com/Heartland/Acres/4031/Lookups.html

Sligo

- County Sligo: Ireland: Lookups by Volunteers
  www.rootsweb.com/%7Eirlsli/lookup.html

Tipperary

- County Tipperary Lookups
  www.rootsweb.com/~irltip2/

Maps

- Ordnance Survey Ireland
  www.irlgov.ie/osi

Pedigrees

- Burke's Irish Family Records
  www.fermanagh.org.uk/genealogy/resources/bureifr.htm

Lists 514 family histories in the book

- Milesian Genealogies
  www.rootsweb.com/~fianna/history/milesian.html
Medieval pedigrees

Peerage & Nobility

- Peerages in Ireland during the 17th Century
  www.rootsweb.com/%7Efianna/surname/dhpeerages.html

- Uasal: a source for Irish Nobility, Heraldry and Genealogy
  ww2.smumn.edu/uasal/noble.html

Scots-Irish

- Our Scotch-Irish Heritage
  members.aol.com/ntgen/hrtg//scirish.html

- The Scots/Irish immigration of the 1700's
  www.zekes.com/%7Edspidell/famresearch/ulster.html
Discussion

- Scotch-Irish Research
  www.genealogy.com/00000384.html?Welcome=991306619
Presbyterian Scots in Ulster

Settlers

- Some of the Earliest Settlers in the Laggan Area of Co. Donegal, Ireland
  thor.prohosting.com/~hughw/laggan.txt

Surnames

- Ancient Irish Surnames
  www.rootsweb.com/%7Efianna/surname/old.html

- An Atlas of Irish Names
  www.ucc.ie/research/atlas
Study of the origins and distribution of surnames

- Common Irish Surnames
  www.pbs.org/wgbh/pages/irish/genealogynames.html
Origins and meanings of 50 surnames

- Common Names in Ireland during the 17th century
  www.rootsweb.com/%7Efianna/surname/dhnames2.html

- Hylit Irish Names
  www.hylit.com/info/Names
Meanings of forenames

- Irish Name Locator: 11th to 16th centuries
  www.rootsweb.com/%7Efianna/surname/name01.html

- Irish Names
  roisindubh.tripod.com
Meanings of first names

- Irish Surnames
  www.cproots.com/surnameorigins/namesystems/namesysir1.htm

- Norman and Cambro-Norman Surnames of Ireland
  www.fortunecity.com/bally/kilkenny/2/irename2.htm
List

- Old Irish-Gaelic Surnames
  www.fortunecity.com/bally/kilkenny/2/irenames.htm

- Surnames Common in Ireland during the 16th century
  www.rootsweb.com/%7Efianna/surname/dhnames1.html

- Surnames Found in Irish Records
  www.from-ireland.net/alphabetsurs.htm

- Using Distribution Studies to Identify the Place of Origin of your Irish Ancestors
  genealogy.org/~ajmorris/dist.htm

- www.Irish Surnames.net
  freepages.genealogy.rootsweb.com/~irishancestors/Surnames_index.html
  General discussion

Cork

- Surnames of County Cork
  homepages.iol.ie/~irishrts/CorkNames.html
  Surname history

Roscommon

- Roscommon Surnames
  www.rootsweb.com/~irlros/surnames.htm
  General discussion of surnames, with lists of common ones

Wexford

- Surnames of County Wexford
  wexford.local.ie/content/28164.shtml
  General discussion

United Irishmen

- Wicklow United Irishmen 1797-1804
  www.pcug.org.au/~ppmay/wicklow.htm

12. Professional Services, Booksellers, etc.

A. Professional Genealogists

If you want to employ a professional genealogist, you should first read

- Employing a Professional Researcher: a practical guide
  www.sog.org.uk/leaflets/researcher.html

Many professional genealogists have their own web page. These are not listed here, but many can be found using gateways such as Cyndi's List (see below). The best way to locate a professional is to consult:

- Association of Professional Genealogists in Ireland
  indigo.ie/~apgi

See also:

- Irish Professional Genealogists
  www.iol.ie/~irishrts/Professionals.html

List of members of the Association of Professional Genealogists in Ireland, and the Association of Ulster Genealogists and Record Agents

- List of Genealogical and Historical Researchers
  www.nationalarchives.ie/gen_researchers.html

Compiled by the National Archives of Ireland

B. Booksellers and Other Suppliers

Alan Godfrey

- Old Ordnance Survey Maps for Ireland
  www.alangodfreymaps.co.uk/ireland.htm

Facsimile publishers catalogue

63

Audio-Tapes

- Audio Tapes.com
  www.audiotaps.com/search2.asp?Search=Ireland

Lists audio-tapes on Irish genealogy available

Books Ulster

- Books Ulster
  www.booksulster.com

Fly Leaf Press

- Fly Leaf Press
  www.flyleaf.ie/

Publishers of Irish genealogy books

Genfindit

- Genfindit: English, Scottish and Irish Vital Records Ordering Service
  www.genfindit.com/index.html

For online birth, marriage and death certificates, census records, *etc.*

Irish Roots

- Irish Roots
  www.genealogy-books.com/books/gpcire.html

Booksellers catalogue

Seanchai Books

- Seanchai Books
  www.seanchaibooks.com

Specialist in new and used Irish books

Ulster Historical Foundation Bookshop

- Ulster Historical Foundation Bookshop
  www.ancestryireland.com/

Subject Index

Administrative Areas 59
Adoptees 17, 22
Adoption 59
Anglo-Irish 59
Archives 8-11
Assizes 58
Audio-Tapes 64

Belfast Newsletter 54
Bible Entries 21
Bibliographies 13, 14, 27, 46
Biographies 21
Births, Marriages and Deaths 37-42, 64
Books 13
Booksellers 7, 64
Burke's Irish Family Records 61
Business Records 42

Casey Collection 59, 60
Cavan Genealogist 61
Cemeteries 17
Census 28, 42-44, 47, 64
Certificates 38, 64
Chapman Codes 60
Chat 6, 28
Civil Registration 37, 38
Clare Champion 54
Clergy 58
Coats of Arms 60
Confirmation Records 44
Convicts, Criminals, Prisoners, *etc.* 56-58
County Pages 5, 26-33

Deeds 21, 44
Directories 44, 45

Easter Rising 60
Ejectment Books 45
Electoral Registers 45
Emigration 6, 10, 15, 21, 45-48
Enclosure Records 48
Ennis Chronicle 55
Estate Records 7, 48, 51

Family History Societies 14, 15
Famine 17, 30, 46, 47, 60
Flax Lists 28, 48
Freeholders 58

Game Licences 49
Gateways 5, 6
Gazetteer 60
Genealogists, Professional 63
General Guides 6, 7
Griffith's Valuation 28, 47, 49, 50, 56

Hearth Tax 50, 51
Heraldry 60, 62
Heritage Centres 11-13
History 6
Homicides 60
Huguenots 59, 60

Immigration 15
Inquisitions Post Mortem 7
Irish Chronicles 60
Irish Link 61
Irish Roots Magazine 61

Jacobites 59
Jews 60
Journals 60

Kenmare Papers 48
Knights 61

Land Records 51
Landowner's Census 51
Landowners 58
Libraries 8-11
Libraries' Overseas 9
Limerick Chronicle 54
Local History 61
Local History Societies 14
Look-Ups 61
Lookups 61
Loyalist Claims 51

Mailing Lists 16-21
Maps 61
Marriage Licences 51, 52
Message Boards 21-25, 28
Monumental Inscriptions 52, 54
Muster Rolls 7, 54

Newsgroups 16
Newspapers 54

O'Lochlainns Irish Family Journal 61
Obituaries 17, 21
Occupational Sources 58

Palatines 15, 17
Parish Registers 38-41, 44

65

Parish Registers, Catholic 38-41
Passenger Lists 46
Patent Rolls 7
Pawnbrokers 58
Pedigrees 61, 62
Peerage 62
Petitions 55
Plea Rolls 55
Police 58
Poll Tax 55
Poor Law 7
Presbyterian Records 55
Publishers 64
Pynnar's Survey 51

Record Offices 8
Registrars 38
Roman Catholics 38, 55

School Records and Registers 55
Scots-Irish 9, 17, 62
Settlers 62
Soldiers 59
Sources 7, 37
Sources, 17th c. 7
Sources, 18th c. 7
Sources, 19th c. 7
Strays 42
Surname Lists 34-37

Surnames 17, 22, 60, 62, 63

Tax Lists 7
Tenants 45, 48
Tithe records 28
Tithes 55, 56
Transportation 56

United Irishmen 63

Web Rings 6
Wills 7, 21, 57
Workhouses 41, 48

Institution Index

Alan Godfey 63
American Irish Historical Society 15
Anthologia Hibernica 38
Archon 8
Association of Professional Genealogists in Ireland 63
Association of Ulster Genealogists and Record Agents 63

Balch Institute 9
Books Ulster 64
British Library 9
Bru Boru Heritage Centre 13
Buffalo Irish Genealogical Society 15

Carlow Research Centre 11
Celtic Connection 5
Centre for Irish Genealogical and Historical Studies 6
Church of Ireland 9, 44
Clare Heritage & Genealogical Centre 12
Clare Library 10
Copac 8
Cork Archives Institute 10
Cork Genealogical Society 15
Council of Irish Genealogical Organisations 14
County Roscommon Family History Society 15
County Tipperary Historical Society 15
Cumann Staire Chontae Thiobraid Arann 15
Curl 8
Cyndis List 5, 34

Donegal County Library 10
Donegal Relief Fund 47
Dublin City Library 10
Dun Laoghaire Library 10
Dun na Si Heritage Centre 13

East Galway Family Historical Society 15
Emigrant Savings Bank 45
Emigration 17

Familia 8
Family History Centres 9
Family History Library 9
Federation of Family History Societies 14
Fianna 6, 16
Fingal County Library 10
Fly - Leaf 64
From Ireland 6, 26-33, 39, 52, 60, 62
Fuller, J. 16

Galway Public Lbrary 10
Genealogical Research Directory 35
Genealogical Society of Ireland 14
General Register Office 37
General Register Office (N. Ireland) 38
Genforum 21
Genuki 5, 14, 16, 26-33, 35
Genweb 5, 16, 18, 21, 26-34

Hawgood, D. 5
Helm's 5
Historical Manuscripts Commission 8
Huguenot Society 60
Hytelnet 8

Immigrant Ships Transcribers Guild 46
Irish American Archives Society 15
Irish Ancestral Heritage Centre 15
Irish Ancestral Research Association 13
Irish Family History Forum 15
Irish Family History Foundation 11
Irish Family History Society 15
Irish Genealogical Society International 15
Irish Genealogical Society of Michigan 15
Irish Genealogical Society of Winsconsin 15
Irish Heritage Centre 11
Irish Migration Resource Centre 46
Irish Palatine Association 15
Irish Roots 64
Irish Times 7, 26-33

Kildare Heritage & Genealogy 10, 12
Kildare Local Studies Dept. 10
Kilkenny County Library 11
Killarney Genealogical Centre 12

Laois & Offaly Family History Research Centre 12
Latter Day Saints 6, 9, 38, 39, 41, 49
Leitrim Genealogy Centre 12
Libdex 8
Library of Congress 13
Limerick City Public Library 11
Linen Hall Library 9
Longford County Library 11

Mallow Archaelogical & Historical Society 15
Mallow Heritage Centre 12
Morris, A. 5

67

National Archives of Ireland 9, 13, 37, 42, 56
National Library of Ireland 9
National University of Ireland 10
North of Ireland Family History Society 15

Offaly Historical & Archaelogical Society 15
Office of the Chief Herald 60
Ordnance Survey 59, 61, 63

Public Record Office 9
Public Record Office of Northern Ireland
  9, 44, 49

Register of Deeds 44
Representative Church Body Library 9

Rootsweb 5, 16, 34
Roscommon County Library 11Royal Irish
  Constabulary 58
Royal Ulster Constabulary 58

Seanchai Books 64
Society of Genealogists 38
Surname Helper 34-37

Tipperary Heritage Unit 11
Tipperary Local Studies Dept. 11
Tipperary North Family Research Centre 13

Ulster Historical Foundation 11, 15, 64
University College, Cork 10

University of Dublin 10
University of Ulster 10
Usenet 16

Valuation Office 49, 57

Walker's Hibernian Magazine 38
Waterford Research Centre 13
West Galway Family History Society 15
Western Family History Association 15
Wexford Genealogy Centre 13
Wexford Public Libraries 11
Wicklow Research Centre 13

Yahoo 16, 17

Place Index

Antrim 11, 13, 18, 22, 26, 35, 38, 42
  Belfast 22, 54
  Island Magee 38

Armagh 11, 14, 18, 22, 26
  Fews 42

Carlow 11, 18, 22, 26, 35, 48, 49, 61
  Fenagh 38
  Killerig 52
  Myshall 38
  Tullow 52

Cavan 18, 22, 26, 27, 38, 57, 61
  Killeshandra 52
  Knocktemple 52

Clare 10, 12, 18, 22, 27, 30, 35, 42, 43, 45, 48, 49, 51, 52, 54-56, 60, 61
  Ardnacrusha 44
  Bodyke 48
  Clonlara 44
  Ennis 44, 45, 55
  Killaloe 51
  Killard 39
  Kilmacduane 39
  Kilmurry 39
  Kilrush 39, 48
  Liscannor 39

Connaught 17, 22

Cork 10, 12, 15, 18, 22, 27, 35, 39, 43, 45, 48, 49, 51, 57, 59
  Ballyneen 39
  Bandon 39
  Berehaven 18
  Desertserges 44, 56
  Enniskeane 39, 44
  Kilcrumper 43
  Kilworth 43
  Kinneigh 44
  Leitrim 43
  Macroney 43
  Mallow 12, 15, 51

Donegal 10, 14, 23, 27, 35, 39, 43, 45, 47-49, 52, 57, 59
  Arranmore 18, 58
  Assaroe 52
  Ballybofey 45
  Ballyshannon 45, 52
  Beagh 49
  Bellanaboy 49
  Bundoran 52
  Carndonagh 23
  Cloghcor 49
  Cloncha 39
  Clonleigh 50
  Commeen 49
  Convoy 50
  Crilly 43
  Culdaff 50
  Derrynacarrow 49
  Donoughmore 50
  Falcarragh 58
  Fallagowan 49
  Finner 52
  Gartan 53
  Garton 56
  Gortgarra 49
  Inishkeeragh 49
  Inishowen 23
  Inver 43
  Killeshandra 53
  Killult 58
  Killybegs 55, 56
  Laggan 48, 62
  Leck 43, 50
  Letterkenny 43, 53
  Lettermacaward 50
  Magheragallon 53
  Mountcharles 43
  Raphoe 39, 51, 55, 57
  Raymunterdoney 58
  Strabane 39
  Stranasaggart 49
  Stranorlar 43
  Taughboyne 51
  Templecarn 43
  Templecrone 49, 50, 56
  Templecrune 58
  Tullaghobegley 53

Down 11, 14, 23, 27, 28, 35
  Lawrencetown 49, 55
  Templecraney 39, 53

Dublin 12, 18, 19, 23, 28, 35
  Dublin 10, 54
  Dun Laoghaire 10
  Fingal 10
  Rathdown 10

Fermanagh 12, 14, 19, 23, 28, 39

Galway 10, 12, 15, 19, 23, 28, 36, 43, 51, 61
   Annoghdown 47
   Aran 19
   Beagh 53
   Cargin 47
   Donagh 47
   Kilcoona 47
   Kilkilvery 47
   Killeany 47
   Killursa 47
   Lettermullen 19
   Moyrus 39
   Shanaglish 53
   Woodford 19

Kerry 12, 19, 23, 28-30, 36, 39, 40, 43, 48, 49, 56, 58, 59, 61
   Abbeydorney, 53
   Ardfert 53
   Ballyferriter 56
   Berehaven 18
   Brosna 40, 50, 53, 56
   Castleisland 40, 50
   Castlemaine 48
   Currauns 50
   Dingle 29
   Keel 40
   Kenmare 48
   Killarney 12, 45, 48
   Killeentierna 50
   Killemlagh 43
   Killorglin 53
   Kiltallagh 40

Lisselton 40
Listowel 50, 53
Nohavel 50
Prior 43
Trughanacmy 40

Kildare 10, 12, 19, 23, 29, 40

Kilkenny 11, 12, 19, 23, 29, 36, 40, 48, 59, 61

Laois 12, 19, 23, 29, 36, 48, 52
   Dysart 53
   Killinard 53

Leinster 17, 22

Leitrim 12, 19, 24, 29, 36, 43, 48, 50
   Leitrim 29

Limerick 19, 24, 30, 36, 40, 43, 45, 48, 50, 54, 61
   Ardagh 53
   Boher 55
   Kilbeheny 53
   Kilfinny 53
   Kilmacow 53
   Kilmallock 48
   Limerick 11, 45, 55, 58
   Murroe 55
   Rathkeale 53

Londonderry 12, 14, 19, 24, 29, 30, 40
   Dunboe 43

Longford 9, 11, 12, 19, 24, 30, 36, 40, 41, 45, 51, 58
   Ballymahon 50
   Edgeworthstown 30, 44
   Newtownbond 53

Louth 19, 24, 30, 48
   Dundalk 57
   Tullyallen 44

Mayo 11, 19, 24, 31, 36, 41, 43, 44, 50, 61
   Ashagower 53
   Ballintober 41
   Bellyburke 44
   Bohola 20
   Burrishoole 44, 45, 53
   Burrishoule 51
   Castlebar 41, 44, 45, 53
   Claremorris 20
   Cuileen 44
   Gorthbawn 44
   Kilgeever 41
   Killadeer 44
   Kilmovee 53
   Kiltimagh 20, 41
   Louisburg 41
   Louisburgh 20
   Newport 44
   Old Head Estate 48
   Roundfort 41
   Swinford 20
   Templemore 50
   Westport 41, 44, 45, 48, 53

Meath 11, 12, 20, 24, 31
   Ashbourne 55

Monaghan 9, 11, 13, 14, 20, 24, 31, 41, 55

Munster 20, 22

Offaly 12, 15, 20, 24, 31, 36
   Arlington 60

Roscommon 11, 13, 15, 20, 24, 25, 29, 31, 32, 36, 41, 43, 50, 51
   Ballykilcline 48
   Baslic 53

Sligo 13, 14, 20, 25, 32, 41, 43, 48
   Ballykilcline 20
   Banada 54
   Castleconnor 41
   Curry 54
   Easky 54, 56
   Grangemoor 54
   Rosser 54
   Sligo 50
   Thurlestrane 54

Tipperary 13, 15, 20, 25, 32, 36, 42, 48, 52, 54, 61
   Ardcrony 54
   Carrick-On-Suir 42
   Clogheen 32

Clonmel 42
Ida 51
Killardry 54
Knocknagoshel 55
Neenagh 58
Offa 51
Outeragh 56

Tyrone 12, 20, 25, 32, 36, 54
   Killeeshil 54

Ulster 5, 10, 13, 17, 22, 62, 64

Waterford 13, 20, 25, 32, 33, 42

Westmeath 13, 25, 33, 37, 43, 60
   Mullingar 42

Wexford 11, 13, 20, 21, 25, 33, 38

Wicklow 13, 21, 25, 33, 37, 42

OVERSEAS

Australia 47, 56, 57
   New South Wales. Sydney 46
   South Australia. Adelaide 46
   Tasmania 56
   Victoria. Melbourne 46

Canada 6, 46, 48
   New Brunswick 47
   Prince Edward Island 47
   Quebec. Grosse Sle 47

Germany 15

New Zealand 47

United States 47, 48, 57, 59
   Buffalo 15
   Chicago 47
   Delaware. Wilmington 47
   District of Columbia. Washington 57
   Iowa 17
   Maryland 47
   Massachusetts 15
   Minnesota. Minneapolis 15
   New Hampshire. Portsmouth 47
   New York 45
   Ohio. Cleveland 15, 17
   Pennsylvania. Philadelphia 9
   Virginia 47
   Wisconsin 15

Vietnam 57